CONTOURS
OF A
DEFAULT FACE

YOUR FACE THAT YOU DO NOT KNOW…

THE FACE THAT TELLS YOUR STORY…

L. A. CHAMBERS.

ISBN: 979-8-89075-662-6

DEDICATIONS

To all those who seek the courage
to pursue their dreams and have good success.

This book is dedicated to you. May it guide and inspire you on
your journey. May it provide the strength and comfort you need
to stay true to yourself and never give up on your dreams.
May it inspire you to love, be a reminder that you are capable
of achieving greatness and that no matter what life
throws your way, you can overcome.

May this book bring you hope, remind you that anything
is possible, and inspire you to continue on your journey of
self-discovery and growth.

Warmly,

L. A. Chambers,

Inspirational Writer.

ACKNOWLEDGMENTS

I would like to express my sincere gratitude to all those who have
supported me during my journey to write this book.

First and foremost, to the utmost from which Love and wisdom
outflows. I would like to thank my family for their endless love
and encouragement; this book would not have
been possible without their support.

I am also grateful to my friends and colleagues who caused me
to be inspired and motivated to take on this journey,
and to encourage all to effect positive changes
for the outward beauty that others will read on us.

Special thanks to everyone who contributed to the making of this
book, and to my publisher, for giving me the opportunity to
share my work and inspirations with the world.

Finally, I am thankful to all my readers who have taken the time to
read this book. I hope that you find it informative, enjoyable, and
rewarding; most of all, I hope you will be inspired to become
cognizant of your true self, and motivated to create the
best version of you, even when you are not looking at yourself.

CONTENTS

PROLOGUE

Once upon a time, there was a young man who was filled with dreams and aspirations; he had hope of a better life but also had obstacles, needs, and unknown traits.

One day, the young man stumbled upon something that changed his life forever: the power of cognizance and volition. With this newfound knowledge, the young man was able to take control of his life and truly discover his true self.

This book is the story of that journey. It is the story of how a person can overcome the odds and find their true self. It is a story of hope, courage, and sheer determination. It is a story of how heightened cognizance and conscious volition can dramatically transform your life, leading to unparalleled success and culminating in a beautiful outward expression.

After all, how you look and the story on your face does matter. This is a story that will inspire you to discover your true inner self. This is a "must read" It is a story that lets you discover things about yourself that you probably did not know, things that will leave you feeling empowered, set you up for success, and ready to take on the world. So, don't leave knowledge on the table.

This book is intended to be a source of inspiration and motivation, to help you recognize and tap into the power of thoughts. It is my hope that by sharing my experiences and insights, I can inspire you to make the necessary changes to create a life you love.

If you're ready, let's begin.

CHAPTER 1

TRAIL OF THOUGHTS

"As a child growing up, I was often told the story of a young man who was offered a chance to ask for anything he desired, and of all the things in the world including wealth, money, and all it could buy, he asks for an understanding heart so he could make wise decisions."

--- *A Coveted Gift*---.

It was mid-morning on a beautiful tropical day. I was assembled in a technical training session on company premises with a bunch of my work colleagues and a professional trainer brought in from overseas. This was a very important training course, directly related to new capital equipment the company acquired as part of a major investment in critical assets.

As members of the technical team, we would be tasked with the responsibility of managing these assets for optimal performance over their lifecycle. Everyone had great expectations from the training and was well-motivated to learn something new. As a result, the atmosphere was packed with good vibes and high energy levels, all pumped for the next phase of our journey.

My colleagues were professionals, but they were a very open and social bunch. They were caring people and would be ready to give a hand without hesitation; however, that company of friends would not hesitate to share a good laugh with each other if you dared. No one was exempted from being "that guy."

The training room was organized in such a manner to facilitate collaboration and information sharing, the tables were laid out in two rows with a face-to-face seating arrangement. I was seated at the South end of the room with a full view of the eastern sky from the second-floor window. It was a such beautiful sunny day. The sun's radiant glow bathed everything it touches in a remarkable way to lift spirits and envelope the environment with delight and a warm embrace, a true conversation starter. As the golden rays of the sun gently kiss the earth, a sense of serenity and optimism washes over us. The clear azure sky stretches endlessly, inviting us to immerse ourselves in its boundless beauty. It was a beautiful day, yet also a day of reckoning.

"A beautiful day, but a day of reckoning I must emphasize."

"It was the day of reckoning because I was made aware
of a face I have, but a face I did not know."

As much as it was our workplace, it was an environment in which making fun of someone and getting a belly full of laughs was not considered bullying by the greater masses. It just seems like the "subtle norm," the lifestyle that is perceived as cool, these folks will laugh at each other to varying social limits, and anything said or done in that environment can easily qualify a candidate. Make no mistake, if you fall victim to such an event, "brace for impact," it's the kind of thing where you give it, and you get it, life goes on. This behavior indirectly motivates people to become "little rascals" but, in a strange way, remain very good friends. While we can argue that not all humor is malicious, it was amazing at times to see colleagues who were the victims of a tease, or "carding" as we often call it, in most cases, also got a nickname as a bonus but end up laughing at themselves and not at all be upset with the offenders.

"Laugh at yourself and find happiness in you."
~~ Inspired ~~.

L. A. Chambers

By the time I snapped out of it and came back to earth, my colleague seated at the table across from me was already totally distracted and chuckling with all eyes on me. In a brief moment of me trying to figure out what was going on, one guy said to me,

"Oh man! You should've seen your face a minute ago."

Things took a turn for the worse as my colleague tried to reconstruct his face, with the contours he saw on my distracting default face in an effort to show me what I looked like a minute ago. The mood suddenly changes from chuckling and sneaky grins to a full outburst of laughter. It was so funny to watch him do the facial expression that even I started to laugh at myself.

What? But seriously, is that really how I looked? I ponder. Of course, I had no idea, but if that's how my default face really looks, I never want to be seen looking like that again. Ever!!

The default face is very difficult, if not impossible, to recreate when you are conscious of yourself, and the contours are nearly impossible to capture with a selfie or posing for a glamour shot, so a person may never get a chance to see their default face and what they truly look like when they are captivated by their thoughts of a lifetime.

"Knowledge and understanding are ingredients to
prosperity, but cognizance is the volition.
Sow choices that make you reap joy."
~~ Inspired ~~.

L. A. Chambers

"It's one thing to find humor in a particular situation,
laugh at yourself and show resilience and mental toughness.
It is another thing to be reflective and self-aware enough
and make the choice to do something about it."

To be cognizant of something is to be aware of it or have knowledge of it; such awareness can be called cognizance. On the other hand, volition is one of the primary human psychological functions. It is the cognitive process by which an individual decides on and commits to a particle course of action or using their will to make conscious decisions.

I recall the words, "Oh man! you should see your face a minute ago." Then I ponder,

"My face a minute ago?" Obviously, the face I had a minute ago is not the face I have right now. Then moment of truth,

"I have a face that I did not know,"

"It's a face that I had never seen."

"It's the face that was telling my story."

"It's the face that shows up without my consent."

"It was my default face."

The water eventually settled, and we were back to the task at hand, but as the training continued, I found myself doing it again, my thoughts "off to the races" wandering away from the immediate task at hand. It's like my mind embarks on an inner journey, detaching from the external world, meandering through memories, and life scenarios triggering the curios distracting gaze. The moment I snapped out of it, I realized my facial expression was of a kind similar to my colleague's reconstructed face.

"Holy cow!" I mouthed to myself as I quickly straightened up my face and scanned the room 360 degrees to see if anyone had just seen that. Luckily, everyone had their head down and was preoccupied with training-related matters. My problem, or so I thought, was "sucking my tongue," and it occurred to me: I had a habit, and this was a habit I had to break.

Tongue sucking is a habit that can make it appear as if you're sucking on hard candy. While a rare habit compared to thumb or finger sucking, tongue sucking can cause discomfort and also make a person feel self-conscious and worried about what people think. Later on, that same day, I found myself in front of a mirror, trying to reconstruct the face that was seen by my colleagues. Of course, I was not the only one with the tongue-sucking syndrome because I know many people who do it when they zone out or are just in their comfort zone. Needless to say, I was able to suck my tongue in front of the mirror. What I was not able to do, however, was to reconstruct those weird facial contours I saw on my colleague's face as he was trying to show me what I looked like. Little did I know that those special facial contours are driven by the thought process. Whatever is on your mind at that time when you zone out, totally captivated by your thoughts, would have a lot to do with how your face looks. It's like a "freeze frame" moment.

"Choose a moment to shine. Let your thoughts gleam from a pure heart."
~~ Inspired ~~.

L. A. Chambers

"Freeze frame" is a term used in vehicle diagnostics, film, or video footage. In simple terms, it's a snapshot of data or a single frame forming a motionless image. This snapshot of data carries a lot to be determined and will tell the story of what is going on at that instance of time as related. In a similar manner, when you zone out, and totally captivated by the thought process, the contours of your face reflect a screenshot of your thoughts, and there's a lot to be determined from the outward expression. That facial expression is a direct replica of your thoughts at this instance of time. Those special facial contours that the owner may never get to see in a lifetime.

One thing to consider from this "freeze frame" moment is that the thought process varies, and one could zone out based on an emotional stimulus that weighs heavily on their mind or zones out from a creative mind or imaginative thought.

Nevertheless, people can and will have different experiences and challenges in life. Put it this way, life is full of ups and downs, and it can be hard to find the joy in our lives when times are tough. But it's important to remember that smiling is an important part of the code of life in this massive and beautiful world. It's something that can help us to stay positive and find beauty in each moment.

When times are tough, it can be hard to force yourself to smile. But the truth is that smiling and having a belly full of laughter can help you to cope with difficult situations. When you allow yourself to be happy, you're sending a signal to your brain that it's okay to let go of stress and negativity, making it easier to stay calm, relaxed, and comfortable as if nothing is worrying you.

In the end, it's important to remember that life has a lot to do with staying alive, finding joy and happiness, and being able cope with what is going on in the environment. Taking a step back, making a deliberate effort to focus on the positives, making a deliberate effort to avoid negative influences, and taking care of yourself will give you the ammunition and drive to overcome challenges, keep your spirits up and win your pursuit. So, "smile through the tough times and keep that code of life alive!"

Fair to say, there are times in our lives when we have been there, we have at some point been exposed to events that make us feel happy, events that make us feel sad, or even a bittersweet moment. Their other events in our lives that make us feel excited and want to jump, shout for joy, or run out into the street undressed, or maybe not, but that Eureka moment will give your feelings wings.

As I am writing this, I choose my words carefully; notice I used the words *"events"* and *"feel."* Think of it this way, events in life are access to your emotions, and people will respond to stimuli in different ways. Some events will make you laugh, cry, shout, or act in a particular way. I recall the story of Archimedes' legendary Eureka moment that "went viral" back in the days.

One version of the story claimed this guy was taking a bath in a tub when he made a remarkable discovery, what is now referred to as the Archimedes principle. His discovery brought him so much excitement that he jumped out of his bathtub and ran down the street to inform the king, shouting, Eureka! Eureka! I have found it. I know you are probably wondering what the heck did Archimedes discover; I promise I will tell you, but let's think about this for a minute, I can't help but visualize a scenario of Mr. Archimedes returning home and sitting down to have dinner, then zone out at the table thinking about this great discovery he has made. Embarking on a thoughtful journey of success and accomplishment the type that cultivate a once in a lifetime emotional response, I am curious to know how this accomplished state of mind, and emotions loaded with excitement and delight would impact his thought process, how would they impact his outward expressions especially the ones that shows up on his face.

"What would his freeze-frame portrait look like?"

"Life events are access to your emotions, so! if you must break.
Break through!"
~~ Inspired ~~.

L. A. Chambers

Archimedes was taking a bath in a tub full of water; he noticed that the water splashed out of his bathtub onto the floor the moment he stepped into it, and the more he climbed into the tub, even more water got splashed out of the tub, he realized that he had made a real mess, but that mess triggered an idea that would help the king on his quest to find the truth about his crown.

This classic tale centers on a king who reputedly entrusted a goldsmith with a bar of gold to fashion a crown for him. When the crown got delivered, the king got suspicious and thought the goldsmith had mixed some of the gold for cheaper silver, but the king had no way of proving his suspicions, so he asked Archimedes to find out whether the crown was made from pure gold without damaging the newly fabricated crown. While Archimedes had his bathtub experience, he reasoned that his body displays a lot of water, so there must be a relationship between the volume of his body and the volume of water displaced because if he was not so big less water would spill on the floor. He took a piece of gold and a piece of silver of the same mass; he dropped the piece of gold into the bucket full of water and measured the volume of water that spilled out of the bucket. He then took a piece of silver, dropped it into the bucket full of water and measure the volume that spill out of the bucket. Although both metals had the same mass, silver had a larger volume, therefore, the silver displaced more water from the bucket than the gold did.

That's because silver was less dense than gold, he reasoned that if the goldsmith had made the crown from pure gold, then the volume displays should be the same as that of pure gold of the same mass. Anyway, it turns out the crown failed the test. When the crown was put into the bucket of water, the volume of water that spilled out of the bucket was different from the volume of water that spilled out of the bucket for the piece of pure gold of the same mass. I can imagine the joy Archimedes felt an overwhelming sense of joy in his heart as he meticulously documented this profoundly happy moment of his life – a breakthrough of unprecedented significance. It was a moment that, beyond a shadow of a doubt, inundated him with delight, fulfillment, and an overwhelming sense of satisfaction. As I envision Archimedes relaying his remarkable narrative, I can picture an enduring smile gracing his face, conveying the sheer magnitude of the story that would leave an indelible and far-reaching mark on the world.

Life events can pull us in multiple directions, often leading us to make life-changing decisions. It can be hard to stay positive in this environment, especially when it seems like the events of life are always throwing curve balls. We can sometimes feel stuck in a cycle of stress and negativity. It can be difficult to break out of it, but if you must break, then breakthrough.

Breaking through negativity, especially when life throws a curveball, is a profound journey of resilience and inner strength. It requires the type of volition and determination to win. Turn on the "never give up mode" this entails the conscious choice to rise above the challenges and setbacks that often accompany unexpected twists in our life's path. It's crucial to acknowledge and be cognizant of negative emotions and thoughts that may arise initially, try to understand their root causes and work towards transforming them into positive energy. It's about developing healthy habits that pushes in the direction of seeing adversity as an opportunity for growth and improvement rather than a roadblock to happiness.

If you must break, then "breakthrough." I must say with emphasis, try to develop or cultivate various coping strategies and support systems. This might involve seeking guidance from friends, family, or professionals, setting realistic goals, and taking one step at a time. It's about learning to adapt and finding the silver lining in challenging situations, external pressures, and societal demands. Fundamentally, "breaking through negativity" is not just about overcoming external obstacles but also about conquering our own inner doubts and fears. It's a reminder that, even in the face of life's curveballs, we possess the power to rewrite our narrative, emerge stronger, and find a renewed sense of purpose and positivity.

At the end of the day, smiling can be one of the most powerful tools we have to help us stay positive, and connected, spreading good vibes to the people we encounter. So, take a moment to smile, make an impact and let your joy radiate out into the world, you never know who you might touch with your smile.

I will be the first to admit that this lesson is one I learnt the hard way. My "freeze frame" moment did not do me much justice, my enigmatic facial expression left much to be desired, and my colleagues did not spare the "rod of humiliation" sharing the spoil and having a belly full of laugh at my expense. But, as I study and delve deep into this concept of the thought process driving the facial expression of the default face, the more I understand that the resulting facial expression of that unseen face offer a fascinating glimpse into the inner workings of the human mind.

These fleeting moments, characterized by vacant stares, mysterious smirks, faraway gazes, or furrowed brows, provide a testament to the multifaceted nature of human cognition. While these expressions may leave much to be desired, it is essential to approach them with curiosity, compassion, and respect, recognizing that they are part of the rich heritage of human experience, habits, and life events, some of which are beyond one's control, especially growing up in demanding environments.

We live in a fast-paced and demanding world, we have our own challenges and success stories, but it is not uncommon to find ourselves lost in our own thoughts, drifting away from the present moment. This intriguing phenomenon, commonly known as "zoning out," can occur at any time and in any situation. While it may seem harmless at first, the enigmatic facial expressions that often follow will not go unnoticed by the onlookers and can leave much to be desired, create suspense, and distractions, or be a delight to behold.

On the other side of the coin, it is a natural occurrence that can happen to anyone, regardless of age, occupation, or background. It is a mental state where our minds detach from the external environment and wander off into a realm of internal musings, daydreams, or deep contemplation. This temporary disconnect can manifest in various ways, affecting our outward expressions in intriguing and often amusing manners, even if you are not prepared. In fact, some individuals may find themselves wearing a slight smirk or grin while lost in thought. This enigmatic smile often hints at a private joke or a pleasant memory that momentarily distracts them from their surroundings. It can be quite amusing to witness these situations, leaving observers to wonder about the source of their amusement and what precisely tickles their fancy.

As I recall what my colleague said to me, "Man, you should have seen your face a minute ago." I now have to wonder how I would match up to Mr. Archimedes during his eureka breakthrough moment. The contours of our enigmatic facial expression would probably be evident, "I tell ya." While mine led me through a humbling situation, his would probably be the delight to the curious onlookers and clear choice for a default face.

Make no mistake, our faces tell stories; it is like an open book, revealing our thoughts, emotions, and experiences to the curious nonparticipating observers. When we zone out or have experience from other states of uncontrolled consciousness, our facial contours undergo fascinating transformations, sometimes taking on an otherworldly quality that we might never see. The lack of conscious control over these facial expressions during these moments can leave others amused or even concerned.

Archimedes created a mess in his bathroom, but that mess created the insight to his "breakthrough moment" and an equally breakthrough principle that would change the world. The contrast here is that a humiliating situation on the other hand, could cause a person to "break" and give up on their endeavors. However, by becoming cognizant of our situation, one can find the courage to breakthrough, and overcome by awakening the dormant power that is within, stepping out of "hurt mode" and reclaiming control.

Cognizance stands as the cornerstone of our consciousness. It is the radiant light that illuminates our thoughts, emotions, and perceptions, allowing us to navigate the intricacies of existence. It is the profound awareness of our own being, the ability to observe and reflect upon our thoughts and actions. I mean if you don't know, then you just don't know, but having knowledge is one of the key elements for prosperity.

We may frequently find ourselves constantly bombarded by a seemingly endless torrent of distractions, scattered in our focus, and sometimes lost in a never-ending whirlwind of thoughts, worries, and regrets. This state of mind often renders us oblivious to various impacting life events, stressors, external circumstances, or even the inherent richness and beauty of the present moment.

The thing about it is that within each of us lies an incredible force waiting to be awakened, "it is the power of volition." It is the innate ability to make conscious choices, exercise personal agency, and shape the course of our lives. It is the driving force behind our actions and the catalyst for transformation. External circumstances may often seem to dictate our path, but we possess the remarkable capacity to break free from the chains of determinism and assert our will to make positive changes in our lives.

Breaking free from determinism may require a deliberate shift in perspective. It calls for a departure from a mindset that sees life as a series of predetermined events to one that acknowledges the boundless potential for personal growth and transformation. We are not mere bystanders in the play of life but active participants, capable of influencing our own destiny.

Far too often, we succumb to the belief that our lives are predetermined, that we are victims of circumstance. But in truth, our power lies in the choices we make and the actions we take. We can endeavor to reclaim the reins of our lives and become the architects of our own reality and break free from the limitations imposed by external circumstances, personal experience, and other impacting events of life that adds no value and is worth dropping anyway.

As our minds wander into the depths of introspection or imagination, our eyes may take on a faraway gaze. It's as if we're peering beyond the physical world, seeking answers, or exploring uncharted territories within our minds. This distant look can be both captivating and mystifying, as observers are left pondering what captivating vistas or profound revelations lie beyond that gaze. It is truly a cognitive mystery.

> *"To gain the kind of knowledge that yields prosperity,*
> *may require a shift in perspective,*
> *a change of mindset,*
> *and a will to persevere."*
> *Inspired.*
>
> *L.A. Chambers*

To add another layer of fascination to the concept, there is more to a person than what meets the eye. It's a curious venture to explore the depths of human cognition and imagination, reminding us of the power of our thoughts and its effect on our outward expression. What if we could cultivate an enigmatic smile that could default to our facial expression? When we get lost in thought, onlookers would get a treat and a moment to appreciate the enigmatic beauty of our inner world.

I imagine it would serve as a gentle reminder of the vastness of human consciousness and the beauty of the inner self, the power of introspection, and the vast array of emotions and experiences that lie beneath the surface. It would open the door for us to appreciate the moments of quiet contemplation and the unique journeys that each individual embarks upon within their own mind. Among the various facial expressions that could arise from the thought process when someone is zoning out, I believe an enigmatic smile would hold a special place. It would be a subtle yet captivating expression that can leave observers intrigued and wondering about the hidden depths behind that serene countenance. Since we do not always have control over this cognitive phenomenon, it is rather important to develop healthy thoughts that can produce life changing results and a beautiful outward expression that we can be proud of.

The ability of a person to become cognizant of their inner drive and find the volition to succeed in life endeavors is a powerful principle that can influence their overall perspective and outward expressions, including that enigmatic smile. It begins with a heightened self-awareness, a deep understanding of one's values, passions, and goals. When individuals are in tune with their true desires and motivations, they can harness an inner clarity to fuel their determination and resilience in the face of challenges. This heightened self-awareness often serves as the catalyst for personal growth and transformation. When we recognize our potential and believe in our ability to achieve our aspirations, we become more driven and focused on our endeavors. We develop a sense of purpose that guides our actions and decisions, propelling us forward even when the path is arduous.

As we strive to attain our goal in life with unwavering determination, we begin to wear an enigmatic smile. This smile is not merely a superficial expression of happiness; it's a reflection of our inner conviction and confidence. It signifies a person who understands that life's endeavors are challenging but embraces those challenges as opportunities for growth and achievement. This smile conveys a sense of self-assuredness and resilience that is both inspiring to others and a testament to the power of determination. The journey of self-discovery and finding the volition to succeed in life endeavors is intrinsically linked to one's outward expressions, particularly that enigmatic smile. It represents a person who has tapped into their inner reservoir of determination, self-belief, and purpose. This smile serves as a beacon of hope and inspiration to those around them, demonstrating that with the right mindset and unwavering commitment, one can find the way through all of life's challenges with grace and, in the end, emerge victorious.

CHAPTER 2

THE SEAT OF INTELLECTUAL INTELLIGENCE

Ever wonder how an idea or thought is generated? Or how ideas are formed through the thought process, and how a tiny jot or a great rush of one's imagination can turn out to be some great wonders of the world?

This marvelous incubation process has been impacting all of civilization since the existence of humanity, and I can't help wondering what the source of this revolutionary, yet imaginative phenomenon is. This thought process never stops; it is a mental process that keeps on going in the mind without any reduction in intensity or strength.

The source of our intellect and intelligence is a multifaceted interplay of our inner selves, encompassing various aspects of our consciousness. These inner dimensions work in harmony, allowing us to engage in intricate thought processes and fueling our capacity to formulate ideas. All in all, this has the potential to lead to significant success and innovative creations. It can also empower individuals to become great leaders and influential figures, and in some cases, even change how the world interacts and collaborates.

This real and somewhat imaginative inner sphere serves as the "cognitive powerhouse" of our intellectual intelligence. It processes information, analyzes data, and generates ideas through a complex web of neurons and synapses. It's the source of logical reasoning, problem-solving, and creativity. Our thoughts, whether conscious or subconscious, originate from the intricate workings of components within this revolutionary inner sphere.

"When we engage in critical thinking, envision possibilities,
or devise innovative solutions, it's our complex inner self
at work, drawing from our knowledge, experiences,
and cognitive abilities."

*"Sow seeds that generate healthy thoughts. They could
germinate ideas that can move mountains."
~~ Inspired ~~.*

L. A. Chambers

Aspects of our complex inner sphere, often considered the seat of our emotions, values, and deepest beliefs, also contribute to our intellectual prowess. Our passions and values can be powerful motivators, driving us to explore ideas and pursue endeavors aligned with our innermost desires. Moreover, our emotional intelligence, an essential facet of the soul, influences our ability to connect with others, empathize, and collaborate. These qualities can be crucial elements for success in various aspects of life.

Other aspects of this incredible revolutionary inner sphere are metaphorically linked to our core desires, aspirations, and play a role in our intellectual endeavors as well. It is where our most profound dreams and goals originate. When we are invested in an idea or a cause, it can provide the unwavering motivation needed to manifest those thoughts into reality. Our deepest convictions and life and purpose often emerge from the depths of our hearts, propelling us to pursue ambitious projects and innovative creations that can reshape the way in which we live, the way in which we interact with the world.

The source of our intellectual intelligence draws upon the synergy of our inner selves and other aspects of our consciousness. It's the harmonious interplay of these elements that enables us to form ideas, think critically, and embark on journeys of discovery that can lead to profound success and transformative change in our lives. Acknowledging and nurturing this intricate connection within ourselves can unlock our fullest intellectual potential. I asked myself, "What do you think the mind is?" "Where is it located?" To satisfy my quest for answers, I went on a survey to get opinions and hopefully a better understanding of what is perceived as the mind. I asked the question: *"What do you think the mind is, and where is it located?"*

The survey responses were:

1. *A set of faculties responsible for all mental phenomena*

2. *Faculties include thought, imagination, memory, will, and sensation.*

3. *A faculty that manifests itself in mental phenomena like sensation, perception, thinking, reasoning, memory, belief, desire, and emotion.*

4. *The mind is associated with the brain. The two are used interchangeably.*

5. *The brain is a physical thing and can be touched. The mind is mental and cannot be touched.*

6. *The mind is conscious, subconscious, and unconscious.*

7. *The organized totality off an organism's mental and physical process and cognitive components.*

What if we all had the ability to search all hearts, and understand every intent of our thoughts? What if we could run a search of all hearts and capture all thoughts in a data management system? Then we could analyze and understand every intent, we could predict all human future behavior and actions before it is carried out or put into action. What kind of world could we create? Maybe one that is free from crime and malicious actions, a world where people are valued, respected, and honored, or create a world of happy people where healthy thoughts are cultivated. While this might not be possible for any one person to understand every intent, or search every heart, it is quite possible for an individual to understand their own hearts, search within themselves, and make choices. The inner man! I went on another survey to get opinions and a better understanding of what is perceived as the inner man, and I set out to ask the question: *"What do you think the inner man is?"*

The survey responses were:

1. *Our inner man is a very spirit man*

2. *The hidden man of the heart*

3. *The innermost aspect of a man*

4. *The soul that refers to our innermost part*

5. *A person's true nature of course self*

6. *The life source of humans*

7. *A consciousness that has no physical form*

8. *Heart or spiritual nature*

9. *Spiritual or intellectual part on man*

Somewhere within the survey responses, I heard the words "the soul." The soul? I pondered for a bit, what is the soul? I asked myself… pretty interesting! I thought, so I started to dig deeper. I embarked on another survey to get more opinions and hopefully a better understanding of what is perceived as "the soul." I set out to ask the question:

"What do you think the soul is as it relates to the inner man?"

The survey responses were:

1. *The immaterial aspect or essence of a human being*

2. *Conference individuality and humanity*

3. *Synonymous with the mind or the self*

4. *Man's will, intellect, and emotion*

5. *Seat of one's memory, conviction, and desire*

6. *Immaterial aspect or essence of human being*

7. *A person's true or internal mind.*

I was amazed by the responses I got from the survey; none of them referred to a physical, tangible thing you can touch, replace, or even see. These actions in the unseen dimension have a long-term influence, impacting our behavior and decisions. Since I set out on my journey to spot default faces, I realize more and more the activities in this invisible dimension find a way to manifest in different ways. Not only do they influence one behavior they form facial contours. The contours tell us a story when you zone out in a moment of time, you are a direct replica of what is active in your head or your command center. None of the responses I got was physical. They all refer to this wild imagination of internal phenomena that cannot be touched or seen. Is this just a wild imagination? Really! A wild imagination?

What is this place that directs our entire life, the seat from where life flows and great wonders of human action are incubated? quite amazing if you ask me. A lot of us just accept the fact that we have a brain, we have a heart, and we have a mind of our own, but the rest we question and even develop religious dogma to satisfy our life demands. But come on! What if we could really know how to tap into this incredible, invisible space and source of energy? What if we really knew how to harness the power within ourselves.

Frequently, I'm caught in a creative whirlwind where inspiration sparks ideas. But there are moments when I'm uncertain how to turn these fleeting sparks into valuable actions. These ideas can be seen as a quest for manifestation, bridging thought with action. They often provoke deep thinking, encouraging us to explore beyond conventional boundaries and delve into our own consciousness.

It's crucial to acknowledge that everyone has a unique story to tell. Our individual lifestyles, environments, and familial backgrounds all act as a dynamic backdrop for the narrative of our lives. These multifaceted influences shape the ideas that take root in our minds, thereby molding our thought processes, which in turn steer our behaviors and actions. Some might dismiss these ideas as mere fleeting thoughts or intellectual ephemera. However, it's important to recognize that these thoughts are not solely neutral or devoid of influence; they can manifest as both positive and negative forces, exerting a profound impact on our behavior and choices in remarkably similar ways.

The Inner Man

The inner man is a concept that has been discussed for centuries and has formed many opinions and interpretations. It is a term that is used to represent the individual's innermost thoughts, feelings, and beliefs. It is kept hidden from the outside world, the part of us that is authentic and honest.

"Ego seeks external approval, but the inner man seeks
"approval of our own conscience."
~~ Inspired ~~.

L. A. Chambers

The inner man is the part of us that is pure and untouched by the outside world. It is our heart and soul, our true self. It is the part of us that holds our most passionate desires and deepest fears, our source of strength and courage. It gives us the courage to face our fears and push through our doubts.

The inner man is often mistaken for our ego. Our ego is the part of us that seeks approval, recognition, and external validation. Our inner man is the part of us that seeks the approval of our own conscience and the validation of our own values. It is the part of us that is driven by our core beliefs and values, our safe haven. I would say it is the place where we can be our true selves, unafraid of judgment or criticism. It is the place where we can be our most honest, be vulnerable and find peace and solace.

"Be true to yourself" is a phrase used casually at times and does not offer much solution to the stimuli driving the issue in the first place. Some use it as compromise or justification for their actions, However, you play this card, the conscience is where the tire hits the road, the part of us that is most real and authentic.

This in itself comes with its own challenges especially as it relates to the struggle for authenticity in a world where conformity often takes precedence, staying true to oneself can be a challenging endeavor. We constantly grapple with external influences or inputs from life events that may lead us astray. Peer pressure, societal expectations, and the pursuit of external validation can obscure the path to authenticity. To nurture the inner self and stay authentic, introspection and self-awareness are crucial. While it's a current trend, societal pressures often force people into predefined roles and norms.

These expectations can push us to suppress our true selves in favor of conforming to societal ideals. For instance, the pressure to pursue a particular career, get married by a certain age, or adhere to specific cultural or gender norms can be immense. Peer pressure, especially during adolescence and young adulthood, can exert a powerful influence on our choices and behaviors. The desire to belong and be accepted by a particular group can lead us to compromise our authentic values and preferences to fit in.

Peer pressure, especially during adolescence and young adulthood, can exert a powerful influence on our choices and behaviors. The desire to belong and be accepted by a particular group can lead us to compromise our authentic values and preferences to fit in. The pressure is on, sometimes it's subtle and designed in clever ways and indirect methods to get your buy-in and to adapt. Over time a person could develop what I referred to as a "media and consumer culture, think about it, mass media, advertising, and consumer culture frequently promote certain lifestyles, body images, and material possessions as markers of success and happiness. These influences can encourage people to emulate these ideals, even if they do not align with their genuine desires or values of the individual. On the other hand, the struggle for authenticity is not just about external pressures but also internal conflicts. Individuals may grapple with their own insecurities, doubts, and the need for external validation. Sometimes it's the kind of self-doubt and need to fit in, these inner battles can further distance them from their true selves.

Be true to yourself! Let this be more than just a casual statement, let it be the volition in overcoming the struggle for authenticity. Navigating the challenges associated with staying true to oneself requires both self-awareness and resilience. The fear of being rejected or criticized by others can dissuade individuals from expressing their true selves. This fear may manifest in relationships, workplaces, or social circles, making it challenging to reveal one's authentic thoughts, emotions, and beliefs. Be true to yourself and develop strategies to help you overcome the struggle for authenticity.

Here are a few tips.

Regularly engage in introspection to understand your values, aspirations, and what genuinely makes you happy. This is self-reflection, it's the type of self-awareness that can serve as a compass when faced with external pressures.

Establish clear boundaries that define your comfort zones and values. Communicate these boundaries assertively to those around you, ensuring that you maintain your integrity.

Seek authentic connections, surround yourself with people who appreciate and respect your true self. Authentic relationships provide a support system that inspires you to stay genuine.

Recognize that vulnerability is a strength, not a weakness. Embrace vulnerability and be willing to share your thoughts and feelings with trusted individuals, allowing for deeper connections, personal growth, self-confidence and a "heads high attitude."

Practice mindfulness, self-care techniques, and routines to stay connected with your inner self. These practices can help you resist external pressures, help you to stay true to yourself, and make choices that resonate with your authentic self.

"Let your conscience set you free" is another phrase I grew up hearing constantly, it is like the "conversational bribe" to get you to do or say the right thing, it's as if you will be pardoned from all your "little selfish ways" you know what I mean! But what does it to truly guard your inner self and let your conscience be free, the part of us we must nurture and protect, the part of us that will lead us to our true purpose in life and lead us to success.

I believe the conscience is synonymous with the voice of the inner man, in other words, the conscience acts as the spokesperson for the inner man. It is the internal moral referee that helps us discern ethical dilemmas and make decisions that align with our core values. When we listen to our conscience, we are, in fact, tuning in to the wisdom of the inner man. This inner voice serves as a guide, urging us to act in ways that reflect our true selves and our beliefs, even when societal pressures pull us in different directions. The "inner man" is the core of our being, our true self, which is often hidden beneath layers of societal expectations, external influences, and ego-driven desires. It is the essence of who we are when we strip away the masks we wear, this inner realm houses our values, and the moral compass that dictates right from wrong.

Building a Skyscraper of Habits

As you can see from my survey, there is no single meaning or definition for this incredible hidden part of our being. I call it the seat of intellectual intelligence. It is a concept that is often connected to personal growth, spirituality, and mental well-being. The concept generally refers to the part of us that is hidden from the outside world, the part that is responsible for our thoughts, emotions, and behavior. It is thought to be composed of many different components, such as our beliefs, values, attitudes, and motivations. These components arc often shaped by our life experiences, and they can have a profound impact on our thoughts and emotions. For example, if we had negative experiences in the past, we could have low self-esteem and struggle to trust others. These negative experiences can shape our thoughts and emotions, as well as our behavior.

People who have had negative or unpleasant experiences such as broken relationships, workplace conflicts, being accused, treated unfairly, being told lies about, or getting a thumbs down on social media sometimes develop unusual external or facial expressions. Think about it, prolonged stimuli create hurting people. People will be hurting inside the walls and outside.

Hurting people go to bed thinking about it, wake up thinking about it, and go to work thinking about it. These thoughts start to form the wrinkles in your face, the shape of the lips, eyes, and cheek muscles. By default, meaning when you are not looking at yourself when in deep thought, or just being focused or attentive, the contours of your face "by default" takes this shape.

The thing about it is that it gets worse with age, as bitterness, unforgiveness, unresolved issues, broken relationships have a way of adding up and become festering as you get older. It's like "building a skyscraper of habits," over a period of time.

Journal your thoughts? Think about it, some people keep a journal. They journal all the bad things that happen to them. Some read it every day, which means they will never heal. "The more time you spend in "thought mode," the more time you allocate to the growth and formation of the muscles that sculpt the contours of your default face."

*"Journal your thoughts? Oh! Just thought I would ask. Build a
skyscraper of healthy habits."*
~~ Inspired ~~.

L. A. Chambers

Luckily, we can learn to better manage our emotions and set up ourselves to better handle difficult situations.

"People who journal happy moments of their lives, by means of logic, if you read them every day, it will reflect or influence your approach to life."

It is believed that by exploring our inner selves, we can gain a better understanding of our own strengths and weaknesses and use this knowledge to make positive changes in our lives.

This incredible source of our creativity and imagination is "there for the taking" We can tap into our creative potential and explore our own unique gifts. This can be beneficial for both personal and professional growth and help us to gain insight into our thoughts, emotions, and behaviors, gain a better understanding of ourselves, build self-confidence, and make positive changes.

Harness the Power

We live in a society where it is becoming increasingly difficult to stay on top of our lives and remain positive in the face of adversity. We are constantly bombarded with negative news, images, and messages, which can make it hard to keep a positive outlook. With these external distractions and demands, it's easy to lose sight of the incredible wellspring of power that resides within each of us. Our inner self, often buried beneath the noise of daily life, is a source of untapped potential waiting to be harnessed.

Think of it as an untapped well of strength, resilience, and creativity, a hidden reservoir of energy and wisdom, waiting patiently for us to delve deeper and unlock its potential. It's the place where our true essence resides, beyond the roles we play in our careers, families, and communities.

"Within this inner sanctum lies an incredible wealth of untapped resources that can help us navigate life's challenges and help us to fulfill our highest aspirations."

To tap into the power of our inner self, we must begin with self-awareness. This means taking the time to understand our thoughts, emotions, and motivations. Through mindfulness practices like meditation, journaling, or even deep introspection, we can peel away the layers of conditioning and societal expectations to uncover our authentic selves. This heightened self-awareness is the key that unlocks the door to our inner strength.

Emotions are a vital component in this pursuit, often serving as signals and messengers that guide our actions and decisions. It is important to develop emotional intelligence, I believe it allows us to harness the power of our emotions, turning them into valuable tools for personal growth and self-expression. Also, if we master the art of acknowledging, understanding, and managing our emotions, we can build resilience and empathy.

When we tap into this creative source, we can innovate, solve problems, and express ourselves in profound ways.

Whether it's through art, music, writing, or any form of creative endeavor, embracing our inner creativity can lead to a deeper sense of fulfillment and purpose. Sometimes life can be filled with challenges and setbacks, and our inner self can be our greatest ally in times of adversity. If we can cultivate inner resilience, that is, the ability to recover from failures, I believe we will be more motivated to tackle obstacles with grace and drive. It's about trusting in our abilities and our capacity to overcome obstacles, no matter how daunting they may seem.

Another component of our inner self is intuition. When rationality alone cannot supply the answers we seek, it is our inner knowledge that leads us.

In the case we can apply the filter to life events, quieting the noise of external influences and listening to our intuition, we can make decisions that align with our true selves and lead to a more authentic and fulfilling life. Just as a garden requires care and attention to flourish, our inner self needs nurturing. Regular practices like self-care, meditation, and self-reflection can help us maintain a strong connection with our inner power. Surrounding ourselves with a supportive community and seeking guidance from mentors or therapists can also aid in this ongoing journey of self-discovery and empowerment.

It's not hard to become a victim to influences that often encourage us to look outward for validation and fulfillment, it's also easy to forget the vast reservoir of strength, wisdom, and creativity that resides within us. If we become cognizant and develop self-awareness, emotional intelligence, creativity, resilience, and intuition, we can unlock the power of our inner self and embark on a journey of self-discovery and empowerment. Take the first step today, embrace the profound potential that lies within you, and allow it to guide you towards a life of purpose, fulfillment, and authenticity.

We all have thoughts and feelings, and it is important to take a step back and recognize them. We can then reframe those thoughts and feelings into positive ones. For example, if we are feeling anxious and overwhelmed, we can reframe it by taking a deep breath and thinking of one thing we are grateful for. While we are at it, don't forget to take care of yourself, it can help you to stay grounded and to better handle any challenges you may face. This can include things like getting enough sleep, eating healthily, and exercising.

Practice the use of affirmations to help you stay positive and focused. Affirmations can be positive statements that you repeat to yourself to stay focused on your goals and what truly matters for your success. Positive affirmations might help you keep your attention on what you want to achieve rather than on what you don't want to achieve.

The Mental Attitude

Here it is! A beautiful masterpiece in progress. I believe the art of developing a positive mental attitude is a masterpiece in progress. It's a canvas where we choose the colors, the brushwork, and the emotions we want to portray. It's an art form that has the power to transform our lives, enhancing our beauty and charisma, reflecting in our outward appearance.

Our thoughts are the raw materials of this artistic journey. They lay the foundation for everything we experience. When we consciously choose to infuse our minds with positivity, we embark on a transformative path. Positive thoughts act as brush strokes, adding vibrant colors to the canvas of our consciousness. This mental palette influences our emotions, actions, and ultimately, our external radiance.

Choose colors of gratitude and resilience, after all, the colors we choose to apply to this masterpiece matter. Gratitude is a radiant shade that adds warmth to our mental canvas. When we appreciate the beauty in our lives, we become artists of contentment. Likewise, resilience is a bold hue that allows us to paint over our setbacks with determination and strength. It is embedded in the powerful life changing concept of cognizance and volition. These colors of gratitude and resilience work in harmony, infusing our mental attitude with grace and fortitude. As we continue the journey in the pursuit of a positive mental attitude, it is important to create a balance and gain understanding of the inner self, using self-compassion as elements of this portrait. Think of self-compassion as the gentlest of brush strokes. It softens the harsh lines of self-judgment and criticism. It reminds us that we are a work in progress, and the art of self-love is a lifelong endeavor. When we treat ourselves with kindness and understanding, our inner beauty blossoms, reflecting in the grace of our outward expression, the part of us we often don't see.

As we continue to paint the portrait of our mental attitude, we discover that the canvas is endless, filled with the limitless potential to create a beautiful expression, one that inspires and uplifts not only us but everyone we touch with our radiant positivity. This beauty extends beyond the surface. It's a language that transcends words, a silent invitation to connect on a deeper level. Radiating positivity will create a space where others feel comfortable, accepted, and valued. Our beauty isn't just skin deep; it's a reflection of the kindness and light within.

As our portrait is unveiled and our mental canvas takes shape, our outward expression becomes the masterpiece on display. A positive mental attitude enhances our radiance in myriad ways. It can be seen in the sparkle of our eyes, the sincerity of our smile, and the confidence in our stride. When we nurture positivity within, it becomes a magnetic force that draws others to us, fostering connections and leaving a lasting impression.

Chanel the energy into the habit of positive thinking, build a big and beautiful skyscraper of healthy thoughts that will help you win in life endeavors. Let's dig into this a bit more and extract some benefits from the preferred habit.

Positive thinking is not just about being optimistic. It is an active process of recognizing and creating opportunities, even in the face of adversity. It is a way to stay motivated and make progress in our life pursuits. It is the belief that anything is possible and that we can achieve our goals.

Positive thinking is a mental attitude that focuses on the good in any situation. It is a way of looking at the world and how we interact with it. It is the belief that if we put our minds to something, we can achieve it. It is the ability to see the potential in a situation instead of the obstacles.

Positive thinking is a conscious choice. We can choose to focus on the good in any situation, even if things seem difficult or overwhelming. We can choose to be hopeful and to keep striving, even when the odds seem stacked against us. We can choose to look for the silver lining in any situation and to seek out solutions instead of dwelling on the problems. It's also about taking responsibility for our own thoughts and actions. We can choose to focus on what we can control instead of worrying about things that are outside of our control. We can choose to be proactive and take the steps necessary to make our dreams a reality.

"Habit is a noun that exhibits from one's attitude, but attitude is the noun that exhibits one's inner thoughts and feelings."
~~ Inspired ~~.

L. A. Chambers

Positive thinking is a powerful tool that can help us to create a better life for ourselves. It is a way to stay motivated and to keep moving forward, no matter what comes our way. By choosing to focus on the good and seek out solutions, we can make progress toward our goals and create a life we love.

It is the act of looking at life in an optimistic and constructive way. It means taking a proactive approach to life, focusing on solutions and opportunities rather than problems and obstacles. It involves looking for the best in every situation. It involves maintaining a positive outlook even when we are faced with difficult or challenging circumstances.

Positive thinking is about focusing on the positives in life and having an attitude of optimism, gratitude, and resilience. It involves being mindful of our thoughts and words and making sure they are constructive and uplifting. Positive thinking is an incredibly powerful tool that can help us stay motivated, improve our relationships, and even boost our physical and mental health. When it comes to choosing and controlling the process of positive thinking, it's important to recognize that it's a choice. We can choose to focus on the positives or the negatives in any given situation. It's helpful to become mindful of our thought patterns.

As I mentioned earlier, the act of reframing our thoughts, when we notice our thoughts drifting down a negative path, we can take a step back and reframe our perspective. Needless to say, this is done in a conscious state of awareness, and we have the power to choose. If you are driven to a state of mild stupor or start to daydream, you have lost the power to choose, and you are now totally captivated by your thoughts.

We can also practice positive affirmations, which are statements that we say to ourselves to encourage positive thinking. These statements can be about any aspect of our lives that we want to improve, such as our career, relationships, or health. Affirmations can be repeated out loud or silently daily, and they can help to shift our thought patterns in a more positive direction.

It's important to remember that positive thinking is a process, and it may take some time to cultivate a more positive attitude. With regular practice, however, it can become a habit and a way of life, developing skyscrapers of healthy habits if you dare.

Our habits are intricately tied to our attitudes, especially when it comes to fostering positive thoughts and a constructive mindset. The way we think and the attitudes we hold often determine the habits we form, and in turn, our habits can reinforce and shape our attitudes. When we maintain a positive attitude and cultivate optimistic thinking, we are more likely to develop habits that reflect these beliefs. For example, if we approach each day with appreciation and an open mind, we may develop the habit of beginning our days with a positive affirmation or journaling about what we're grateful for. These behaviors, in turn, reinforce our good attitude and set the tone for the rest of our day.

"Conversely, negative attitudes can lead to destructive habits that perpetuate pessimism and self-sabotage."

If we habitually engage in negative self-talk or ruminate on our failures, it can result in behaviors such as procrastination or avoidance. These habits further solidify our negative attitude and can create a self-fulfilling cycle of negativity. Recognizing this connection between attitudes and habits is essential for personal growth and well-being.

"Our habits are the building blocks of our daily lives, and they often originate from the attitudes and beliefs we hold."

Our attitudes serve as the foundation upon which our habits are constructed, and our habits, in turn, have a profound impact on reinforcing and shaping our attitudes over time.

"Consider, for instance, the individual who approaches life with a generally optimistic attitude." Such a person tends to see opportunities in challenges, views setbacks as learning experiences, and maintains a hopeful outlook. This positive attitude, consciously or unconsciously, guides them towards forming habits that reflect these beliefs. They might habitually engage in activities like daily affirmations, gratitude journaling, or seeking out opportunities for personal growth.

"These habits reinforce their positive attitude and act as daily reminders of their constructive state of mind."

"On the contrary, someone with a predominantly negative attitude may develop habits that align with their pessimism."

Constantly dwelling on past failures, impacting bad experiences, or always expecting the worst outcomes can lead to habits like avoidance, procrastination, or self-criticism. These habits, in turn, further cement their negative attitude and can create a self-reinforcing cycle of negativity and unwanted stress.

"Recognizing this intricate connection between attitudes and habits is a powerful tool for personal development."

It implies that we have agency over our mindset and can consciously cultivate positive attitudes by deliberately choosing and nurturing habits that support our desired outlook.

"Making small, consistent changes in our daily routines and thought patterns, we can gradually shift our attitudes towards a more positive and constructive mindset."

Consciously working on our attitudes and fostering a positive outlook will help to set us up for a breakthrough. The type of breakthrough that can go viral, change a home, change a community, or change the world, positively influencing others to win at their endeavors as well. As time goes by, we can gradually develop a skyscraper of habits that align with our desired state of mind and lead to a more fulfilling, positive, and optimistic life. Having the mental attitude to win in life and conquer challenges is intimately tied to the development of healthy habits over time. A positive and resilient mindset is often the driving force behind our ability to persevere through difficulties and achieve our goals. Developing these empowering mental habits is a gradual process, but it can be significantly influenced by consistent, positive behaviors and lifestyle choices.

Healthy habits, such as setting clear goals, maintaining a growth-oriented mindset and practicing self-discipline, can lay the foundation for a winning mental attitude. When we establish the habit of setting and working toward our objectives, we become more focused and driven in our pursuits. Over time, this helps us build a sense of purpose and direction, which is essential for overcoming obstacles that approach us. Similarly, a growth-oriented mindset, characterized by a willingness to learn from failures and view challenges as opportunities for growth, can be cultivated through habit. When we consistently approach life with a mindset that values resilience and learning, we are better equipped to tackle adversity. This practice of viewing failures as stepping stones to achievement promotes a winning mentality that sees every difficulty as an opportunity to evolve and better.

Self-discipline and commitment to these habits reinforces our mental attitude to win. When we make a habit of prioritizing our goals and consistently putting in the effort required, it strengthens our determination and resolve. This steadfast commitment to our aspirations creates a resilient mental attitude, prepared to face the challenging obstacles life throws our way.

Developing a mental attitude to win in life and overcome challenges is closely linked to the cultivation of healthy habits over time. These habits empower us to set and pursue our goals, maintain a growth-oriented state of mind, and practice self-discipline. As these practices become embedded in our everyday lives, our mental attitude shifts to one that is well-prepared to overcome adversity and grab chances that lead to success.

Condition of the Heart

The heart is also linked to our thoughts. It is believed that our thoughts are created in the heart and sent out into the world. Our heart has the capacity to receive and send out energy. This energy can influence our thoughts and emotions, as well as our physical well-being. It is thought that the heart is the center of our being and that it is intimately connected to the universe. This connection allows us to access universal wisdom, which can give us insight into our lives and our relationships. It is the part of us that is linked to our higher consciousness and is the source of our motivations and passions. When we are in touch with the depths of our inner self, we can access our inner wisdom and gain insight into matters of the heart.

Wow! This incredible facet of our being is intertwined with so many aspects of our lives. It provides love and vigor. So, consider this: if we are able tune into our hearts, we have the possibility of unlocking deep wisdom and acquiring insight about ourselves and our relationships. Building a skyscraper of healthy habits and behavior also plays a key role in the condition of our hearts. If we are living a lifestyle of negativity, it can be difficult to experience love. When we engage in unhealthy habits such as substance abuse, it can lead to a disconnection from our inner self and a lack of self-love. On the other hand, when we engage in positive habits and behaviors, it can lead to a connection with our inner self and a greater capacity to love.

The condition of the heart reflects our thoughts, habits, and behavior. If we focus on positive thoughts, engage in healthy habits, and practice positive behavior, then we can open our hearts to the beauty of love. Love is a powerful emotion that can bring us joy and contentment. With the right care and attention, we can all experience the power of love.

Throughout history, the heart has been universally recognized as a symbol of life, vitality, and the core of our being. Beyond its physical function as a vital organ, the heart holds a profound metaphorical significance. It is considered the wellspring of life, symbolic power, spiritual essence, and shapes our existence. It is often associated with love, compassion, courage, and the seat of emotions. The heart is seen as the center of our being, transcending the boundaries of language and culture to connect us on a fundamental level as human beings.

In many spiritual and philosophical traditions, the heart is considered more than a physical organ; it is believed to be the dwelling place of our soul or spirit. It is seen as the gateway to higher consciousness, inner wisdom, and a source of divine connection. The heart's intuitive intelligence guides us in aligning our thoughts, emotions, and actions with our true essence.

Emotions are often felt in the heart, and it is through the heart that we experience the depths of joy, love, compassion, and empathy. It acts as a conduit for expressing and experiencing the full range of human emotions, allowing us to forge deep connections with others and ourselves. It is in the heart that we find solace, healing, and the capacity to forgive, thus nurturing our emotional well-being.

"The heart, both symbolically and spiritually, holds the power of being the wellspring of life, we are encouraged to guard our heart, because everything you do flows from it."

It is the seat of our emotions, the center of love and compassion, and a gateway to higher consciousness. its significance extends beyond the individual realm and permeates our relationships with others. It is through heartfelt connections that we often experience the richness of human interactions.

It serves as the source of empathy, understanding, and the ability to forge deep bonds. It allows us to connect with others on an authentic level, fostering love, compassion, and unity.

The right condition of the heart is the fertile soil from which healthy thoughts naturally sprout and good habits flourish. It's a state of inner harmony and emotional well-being that serves as the wellspring of positivity in our lives. When our hearts are filled with love, gratitude, compassion, and contentment, our thoughts become infused with these virtues, leading to the formation of nurturing and constructive mental habits.

Healthy thoughts are like seeds planted in the fertile soil of a content and compassionate heart. When we think positively, we are more likely to embrace a growth-oriented frame of mind, seek opportunities for self-improvement, and respond to challenges with resilience rather than defeatism. These healthy thoughts give rise to constructive habits, such as daily affirmations, gratitude practices, and acts of kindness, which, over time, become an integral part of our daily lives.

This highly desired beautiful outward expression, especially on our faces, is the natural consequence of this inner alignment. When our hearts are at peace, our faces radiate warmth and serenity, often in the form of a gentle smile. This smile is not merely a reflection of happiness; it's a manifestation of the positive inner state we've cultivated. It communicates to the world the beauty of a heart in harmony with itself and the transformative power of nurturing our inner selves.

"The right condition of the heart is the catalyst for a
cascade of healthy thoughts, virtuous habits,
and a radiant outward expression that
can light up our own lives and inspire others."

CHAPTER 3

THE UNSEEN REALM
OF UNCONTROLLED CONSCIOUSNESS

Have you ever wondered what goes on in your head when you cry or just cracking up with a belly full of laughter? I thought about it all the time. What is the body chemistry for sadness and laughter? What allows tears to flow naturally, and where does all the "magical eye water" come from? Is there a well or stream of water in your head that suddenly decides to burst open when you are hurting, overwhelmed or emotionally touched?

Think about it, what is the source of the laughter bubble? When activated, it can go on uncontrollably for a while to the point of tears and unintentional body gestures. These are real responses to one's emotions, and they are the same irrespective of ethnic background or other social classification. Looking out of space or gazing into space is often referred to as daydreaming. What is going on in your mind at this time? Is your body held hostage by your thoughts? Is your mind in a state of shock? I have been caught gazing into space before and recovered with the snapping finger technique. This is a unique experience when a person's Daydreaming moment is interrupted by someone snapping the fingers in front of the person's face while saying the words "come back to earth."

When you are caught in this state, people will say something like, "What are you thinking about now?" response always or most often is "nothing." But the fact is that you are, do you know what you look like at that moment when you are captivated by your thoughts. What you are thinking about has totally captured your self-awareness.

Uncontrolled states of consciousness are states of awareness that are not under the control of the individual experiencing them. They include altered states of consciousness such as sleep, dreaming, trance, hypnosis, and hallucinations. Daydreaming, zoning out, thinking out loud, doodling, and sometimes tongue-sucking are all forms of uncontrolled state of consciousness. They can be useful tools for relaxation, problem-solving, and creativity, but they can also be a source of distraction for you and the audience across the training room or board room table. As funny as it may sound, an altered and uncontrolled state of consciousness also creates altered and uncontrolled facial expressions. It is important to be aware of how these states of consciousness affect a person's ability to focus, achieve their goals and ultimately win in their life endeavors.

"A snap of the fingers to your face may take you back to earth, but your thoughts will take you back to a realization of your true self.

~~ Inspired ~~.

L. A. Chambers

In everyday life, people are usually in control of their consciousness. We are aware of our surroundings, our thoughts, and our feelings. But sometimes, we can lose control of our consciousness. This can result in an altered state of consciousness that can range from mild disorientation to extreme and intense trance-like states.

In some cases, entering an uncontrolled state of consciousness can be beneficial. For example, certain types of meditation often involve entering a trance-like state in order to achieve a deeper level of relaxation. As human beings, we are often unaware of our own uncontrolled consciousness.

"This part of our minds is hidden from us, operating on a level that is beyond our conscious understanding. It is a realm of thought processes and emotions that are often difficult to access but which play a powerful role in our lives."

The unconscious mind is the source of our instinctive reactions and behaviors. It is part of our mind that takes over when we are in a state of fear or stress or when we are in the presence of something unfamiliar. It is the part of us that makes us act and react without thinking, and it is this part of us that can be so difficult to control. It is also the source of our creative ideas and our ability to think independently and think "outside of the box" as you know it.

It is the part of us that gives us the ability to think of creative solutions and come up with innovative ideas. It is this part of our mind that can lead us to new discoveries and new perspectives on life. This source of our spiritual connection is the part of us that can help us to tap into our higher consciousness and gain insight into our true purpose in life. The source of our emotions is this part of us that can open us up to a deeper understanding of human experience.

"It is this part of us that can truly help us to find our way in life and also help us to become the best version of ourselves."

The unconscious mind is a powerful force within us. I believe if we could learn to understand and control It, we would have given ourselves a dynamic tool that can help us to become better, more effective, and more successful. With the right understanding and control, we could use the power of our uncontrolled consciousness to help up reaching our full potential.

Zoning Out

Have you ever experienced zoning out? It's that feeling of being completely lost in your own thoughts and totally unaware of your surroundings. Zoning out is a type of uncontrolled state of consciousness that can be beneficial but also have other undesired consequences to the individual experiencing it.

When someone is zoning out, their thought process is often characterized by a lack of focus and direction. Thoughts can drift from one topic to another, or they can become fixated on one particular idea. During this period of zoning out, the person's facial expressions may become vacant and expressionless, as if they are in a trance-like state.

This uncontrolled state of consciousness can be a sign of stress, anxiety, or mental fatigue. It can be a way for us to cope with overwhelming emotions or situations. It can also be a sign that our minds need a break from the pressures of everyday life. The benefits of zoning out can include improved concentration, deeper understanding of a problem or situation, and better appreciation for life in general. Zoning out can also be a great way to relax and reduce stress. On the other hand, zoning out can create feelings of confusion and disconnection from the world. It can also lead to distractions and lack of productivity. Regardless of the potential outcomes, it can help us to become more aware of our inner thoughts and feelings, enabling us to better understand ourselves and our environment. So, if you ever find yourself zoning out, take the opportunity to turn inwards and reflect on your innermost thoughts and feelings.

It is a natural occurrence that happens to everyone, regardless of age, occupation, or background. It is a mental state where our minds detach from the external environment and wander off into a realm of internal musings, or deep contemplation. This temporary disconnect can manifest in various ways, affecting our facial expressions in intriguing and often amusing manners.

Let's try this again, does it make you curious?

As our minds wander into the depths of introspection or imagination, our eyes may take on a faraway gaze. It's as if we're peering beyond the physical world, seeking answers, or exploring uncharted territories within our minds.

"Wow! This is deep, this distant look can be both captivating and mystifying, as observers are left pondering what captivating vistas or profound revelations lie beyond that gaze."

The art of zoning out is a fascinating journey into the uncharted waters of our consciousness. It's a terrain where both positive and negative thoughts can emerge, and where our awareness plays a crucial role in shaping our outward expressions. Navigating these mental currents with mindfulness and intention, we can harness the power of positivity and reduce the impact of negativity on our mood and demeanor.

Zoning out, when guided with mindfulness, becomes a transformative practice that enhances our overall well-being. It's about allowing our minds to wander freely, sometimes into the realm of both positive and negative thoughts. How we navigate this mental terrain has a profound impact on our outward expressions, especially when our consciousness is left unchecked.

Zoning out, in its uncontrolled form, often gets a bad rap. We may perceive it as unproductive or even disruptive, particularly when it leads to negative or distracting thoughts. In this state, our minds can become a battlefield of conflicting ideas, worries, and regrets. The uncontrolled currents of consciousness can drag us into a whirlpool of negativity that's difficult to escape.

These are what I would refer to as the "hidden influence of negative thoughts," when left unchecked during zoning out, negative thoughts can cast a shadow on our mood and behavior. These thoughts might stem from past regrets, anxieties about the future, or self-doubt. When we find ourselves dwelling in these negative territories during our mental wanderings, they can seep into our outward expressions, leading to a gloomy countenance, withdrawn posture, and a general aura of negativity. Conversely, zoning out can also lead to positive thoughts when we least expect them. Creative ideas, flashes of inspiration, and moments of gratitude can all emerge spontaneously during these mental journeys. These positive thoughts can, in turn, influence our outward expression, leading to a smile, a sense of calm, and a general aura of positivity. How is that for a default face? How is that for an outward expression to share with the curious onlookers?

Recognizing the importance of awareness, the art of zoning out lies not just in the act itself but in how we navigate its currents. Awareness is the compass that guides us through this uncharted mental terrain. By developing self-awareness and the ability to discern when our thoughts are gravitating towards negativity, we empower ourselves to consciously shift the trajectory of our consciousness towards a more positive outlook. This mindful redirection of our thoughts not only restores our control over our mental landscape but also enables us to proactively shape our perspective and responses to life's challenges, ultimately fostering a more harmonious and resilient state of mind. It's like harnessing the power of mindfulness and using it as a tool in the art of zoning out. It could allow us to observe our thoughts without judgment and gently guide them in a more positive direction. With mindfulness, we can acknowledge negative thoughts without getting entangled in them, and we can amplify positive thoughts, allowing them to flourish.

"A balanced expression of consciousness is most desirable."

When we strike a balance between mindfulness and zoning out, we gain a deeper understanding of the profound impact of our thoughts, our outward expression, our emotional state, and how we present ourselves to the curious onlookers.

Daydreaming

Daydreaming is often associated with zoning out. This is a form of mental disengagement in which a person becomes unaware of their surroundings, and their thoughts wander from the current moment into a curious blank stare.

It can be a way to escape from reality, whether we are cognizant of it or not; daydreaming is considered an uncontrolled state of consciousness in which the mind is left to wander and explore its own thoughts and ideas.

"While daydreaming can be a beneficial and creative experience, it can also be detrimental to our productivity and can lead to distraction and negative thought patterns."

Daydreaming can be a sign of an active and creative mind, as it allows the individual to explore ideas and concepts that they may not be able to access while in a controlled state of consciousness. It can also be a great source of stress relief, as it allows the individual to escape from their current reality and explore more pleasant or interesting thoughts.

The thought process during daydreaming is often characterized by "stream of consciousness" thinking, meaning that the thoughts come and go in an uncontrolled and often unpredictable manner. The thoughts may be random and unrelated or they may be related to the individual's current situation or mood. However, some of the common facial expressions that one may observe in a daydreaming individual include a blank, unfocused stare or a relaxed, contented expression. It is important to be aware of the thoughts that come to mind during daydreaming and to ensure that they are positive and productive. Additionally, it is important to be aware of the facial expressions that one expresses while daydreaming, as they can be indicative of the individual's current mental state.

"In other words, your face is telling your story of what is in your inner self and taking you over in a moment of time."

It is a natural and spontaneous mental activity where our thoughts wander away from the immediate tasks or surroundings and delve into an imagined world or scenario. It involves a form of self-generated, internal storytelling where we engage in thought processes unrelated to what is going on around you. Daydreams encompass a spectrum of mental wanderings, spanning from basic contemplations of future aspirations and recollections of bygone days to intricate daydreams involving imaginative fantasies and inventive brainstorming. The nature of these mental excursions is shaped by a blend of our habits, way of life, and the intricacies of our thought patterns.

Our habits play a significant role in shaping the content and frequency of our daydreams. For example, individuals who have cultivated a habit of mindfulness and staying present in the moment are less prone to excessive daydreaming, as they have trained their minds to focus on the here and now. Conversely, those with a habit of letting their thoughts wander freely may find themselves daydreaming more frequently. The nature of our daydreams can also be influenced by our habits. If we regularly engage in activities that require creativity, such as art, writing, or problem-solving, our daydreams may be filled with imaginative and inventive scenarios.

Lifestyle factors also have a profound impact on daydreaming. Stressful or monotonous lifestyles can trigger daydreams as a form of mental escape or coping mechanism. These daydreams might serve as a way to explore alternative, more pleasant realities, providing temporary relief from the endless pressures of daily life. Additionally, our social interactions and exposure to various stimuli in our environment can shape the content of our daydreams. Conversations, media consumption, and the people we interact with can introduce new ideas and scenarios into our daydreaming repertoire.

"In essence, daydreaming is a fascinating reflection of our inner thoughts, influenced by our habits and lifestyle."

It serves as a window into our desires, fears, and aspirations, providing a valuable opportunity to understand and, if needed, redirect our mental processes towards more positive and constructive patterns.

Doodling

What if abstract art could talk, or if there was a scientific process to decode a *"masterpiece"* of an absentminded scribble to interpret the thought process of a Doodler. I found myself creating *"masterpieces"* at times and have also seen them done by others who have absolutely no idea of what is going on when they are doing it, what just happened or in fact, what they just did.

Doodling is an art form that is deeply rooted in the unconscious state of consciousness. It is a creative process that allows our minds and fingers to wander freely without any sense of constraint, direction, or coaching. When doodling, we allow our minds to wander and explore the depths of our imagination. This form of creative expression allows us to explore our thought process and facial expressions in an uncontrolled, spontaneous way. This uncontrolled state of consciousness allows us to be more open to inspiration and new ideas. It is an incredibly freeing experience that can unlock hidden potential in our minds. The process of doodling requires us to draw whatever comes to mind without overthinking or judging. It is a form of active meditation that allows us to express our thoughts and emotions in a creative way. Doodling can be a great way to express our feelings and develop new ideas, as it helps us to think more freely. This is great, and sometimes it gives me a good feeling to see what I scribbled. More interesting is what I scribbled on. And to be honest, it's not always done on canvas, in art books, or in a nicely framed medium. I have seen it done on napkins, payment receipts, book covers, and even the jeans worn at the time. Just amazing!

This is a free expression of thoughts in a moment of time, an expression of one's true self expressed in the masterpiece of art. But what about clarity? What if we find a way to harness the interpretation of this masterpiece, of what could be considered abstract art and gain insight into the cognitive benefits? What if we could help people to understand more about themselves, create different levels of awareness of their inward state and outward expressions? That would be a magnificent game changer. This "abstract art form" in my opinion is not at all abstract, it can help us to explore our own thoughts and feelings without fear of judgment or criticism. Through this creative practice, we can learn to express ourselves more freely and authentically, allowing us to become more aware of our inner selves.

On the other hand, this creative practice can also create a facial expression that a person may never see in a lifetime unless is captured on camera or someone is brave enough to attempt a reconstruction of those contours on their own face, in an effort to show you how you look a minute ago. Lol.

Overall, doodling is a powerful practice, it can help us to explore our thought process, facial expressions, and emotions in a creative and meaningful way. The art form is far from a mindless pursuit. It's a portal to our consciousness, where positive and negative thoughts coexist. How we doodle and what emerges on the pages or surface, can reveal our inner world and influence our outward expressions. With mindful doodling, we can harness this art form to navigate our thoughts, transform negativity into positivity. It's a unique window into our consciousness, a canvas where our thoughts, both positive and negative, come to life. How we doodle and what emerges on the surface can offer profound insights into our inner world and impact our outward expressions, especially when our consciousness is uncontrolled.

We unleash the power of our subconscious mind in this uncontrolled state, our thoughts take on a life of their own, flowing from our innermost feelings and beliefs. It's here that the positive and negative aspects of our consciousness often find their voice, as we sketch out the landscapes of our mind.

The content of our doodles can be a mirror reflecting our thoughts and emotions. Positive thoughts might manifest as vibrant colors, graceful lines, and uplifting shapes. These doodles can express joy, inspiration, or gratitude, subtly affecting our outward expressions by enhancing our mood and body language.

On the flip side, negative thoughts may also emerge through our doodles. Shapes may become jagged, colors dark and somber, and the overall composition chaotic. These drawings can act as a warning sign, highlighting underlying stress, worries, or anxieties that might be lurking in our consciousness, impacting our mood and outward demeanor, especially the ones that show up on our face.

Doodling isn't just a passive reflection of our thoughts; it's a canvas for exploration and transformation. When we become aware of negative patterns in our doodles, we have the opportunity to address and redirect those thoughts. It's a visual form of self-reflection that can lead to personal growth and a shift towards positivity. It is a creative outlet for processing and transforming negative thoughts into positive ones. Think about it for a minute, by giving form to our fears or concerns on paper, we externalize them, making them more tangible and manageable.

This creative act can be cathartic, enabling us to move past our negativity and present a more positive face. So, the next time you find yourself doodling, take a closer look at what you're creating, you might discover a world of possibilities on paper. Doodling is a fascinating state of uncontrolled consciousness that provides a unique window into our thought processes and habits. When we engage in doodling, we often allow our minds to wander freely, giving rise to spontaneous and unstructured drawings or patterns. This seemingly purposeless engagement is, in reality, a manifestation of the complex inner mechanisms of our thoughts, laying bare our inner contemplations, emotions, and yearnings of our subconscious.

"It can be a tool for self-reflection and self-expression."

The results of these seemingly random scribbles and drawings can offer insights into our current mental state, concerns, and preoccupations. The images that emerge on the page may not always be immediately recognizable, but they carry the imprint of our inner thoughts and feelings. For instance, a doodle filled with geometric shapes might suggest a mind seeking order and structure, while a page covered in flowing lines and curves could reflect a desire for freedom and fluidity in thought.

The curious look on your face when you start to doodle can be telling. It's an expression of curiosity and exploration, a willingness to delve into the unknown corners of your mind.

Doodling can serve as a form of creative meditation, where your mind roams freely, unburdened by the constraints of logic and structure. As you try to interpret your doodles and connect them to your emotions and experiences, you may uncover hidden insights about yourself that you did not know and gain a deeper or clearer understanding of your thought patterns and lifelong habits. It is a captivating journey through the landscapes of our consciousness. It is a process that bridges our inner world with the external one, allowing us to express, explore, and interpret our thoughts and emotions in a way that is both introspective and artistic. Let's embrace this creative practice, in so doing, we may unlock the stories hidden within our doodles and possibly gain a fresh perspective on our own inner workings.

"Choosing to live a healthy lifestyle encourages habits of mindfulness and self-reflection."

These practices can enable us to connect with our thoughts and emotions on a deeper level, fostering self-awareness and emotional intelligence. When we doodle with a clear mind and a heart in balance, our creative expressions become more authentic and meaningful, reflecting the beauty of our inner harmony. A radiant smile during the act of doodling would be the most desirable, it would signify the joy and fulfillment that comes from living a well-rounded and healthy life, where physical health, emotional well-being, and a positive thought process converge to create a harmonious and expressive existence, "our masterpiece."

Thinking Out Loud

Have you ever been lost in thought, often to the point where you start talking to yourself? You're not alone.

This phenomenon, known as "thinking out loud," is a common occurrence and often happens to people when they are in an uncontrolled state of consciousness, with a lot on their mind.

Growing up generally, and when in certain social circles, I often hear people refer to this as the "first sign of madness," of course it was just for laughs. I never really stop to think of the science of it, or the phenomena that is driving this practice. I find myself doing it on many occasions especially when something is bothering me or if I am trying to solve a problem, it's like "brainstorming myself," with very little concerns of the cause.

I remember on one occasion; life circumstances led me to resign from a job that I liked doing. As I was in the process of writing the resignation letter, I found myself talking out loud, asking myself, "what the heck are you doing man?" as I push the backspace button on my computer keyboard deleting the words I just typed. Looking back as I write this book, I realize how funny that must have been, given the amount of time I ask myself the "madness question" as I push the backspace key.

In fact, it was a life-changing decision I had to make, and let me tell you, the feeling of uncertainty and the overwhelming curiosity of the future effects almost got the best of this cat.

Nevertheless, as I deep dive into my research it started to make more sense and help me to garner a better understanding of the subject matter "I am now able to pick sense out of nonsense talk." PS. If there is any consolation, it's not a sign of madness.

Thinking out loud is a type of verbal self-talk. It usually happens when someone is deeply engrossed in their own thoughts and ideas and is unable to control the words coming out of their mouth. It's a form of verbal processing where the speaker is trying to make sense of their thoughts and emotions or to work through a problem. It's also a form of self-expression, allowing the speaker to express their innermost thoughts and feelings without censorship. Thinking out loud is a natural part of the thought process. It's a way to organize and make sense of the information that's swirling around in our heads. It can also help us to clarify our thoughts, as the act of speaking out loud can help to bring our ideas into alignment and sharper focus.

It's important to note that thinking out loud can also be an indication of a deeper mental health issue. It's not uncommon for people who are struggling with depression, anxiety, emotional hurt, or other mental health issues to find themselves talking out loud to themselves as a way of coping with their inner turmoil. If this is the case, it would not be a bad idea to talk to somebody about it or seek professional help, after all, if it helps then tell it out loud. However, we all talk to ourselves from time to time, whether it's murmuring about a forgotten task or giving ourselves a pep talk before a big event. This internal dialogue is like a constant stream of consciousness, where our thoughts, both positive and negative, find a voice. But have you ever considered the impact of talking out loud, especially when our consciousness is uncontrolled? It represents a distinctive avenue for self-expression that has the potential to unveil the depths of our inner world, mold our thought processes, and even exert an impact on our external comportment.

The art of thinking out loud is a heartfelt dialogue with our inner world. Whether it's uncontrolled musings, mindful self-talk, emotional response, or problem solving, what we say to ourselves influences our thoughts, emotions, and outward expression.

When we talk out loud to ourselves, we often unleash the unfiltered stream of our consciousness. It's an uncontrolled release of thoughts and emotions, much like a river that meanders through various landscapes. In this state, both positive and negative thoughts can surface, often competing for our attention. Positive self-talk can be a tool for self-empowerment. When we engage in uplifting conversations with ourselves, we bolster our self-esteem, boost our confidence, and nurture a positive mindset. This positivity can manifest in our outward expression, radiating through our smile, posture, and overall demeanor.

Conversely, negative self-talk can cast a shadow on our consciousness. When we indulge in self-criticism, doubt, or self-deprecating thoughts, our inner dialogue can become a breeding ground for negativity. This darkness may creep into our outward expression, affecting our body language, facial expressions, and even our interactions with others. Thinking out loud can also be an emotional release valve. When we voice our thoughts and feelings, it's like unburdening ourselves of emotional baggage. This cathartic process can bring relief and help us manage stress, anxiety, or other negative emotions that might otherwise impact our outward expressions negatively. Talking to oneself is a common and often misunderstood behavior that can provide insights into our uncontrolled state of consciousness. When we engage in this practice, we externalize our thoughts, making them more tangible and accessible for self-reflection. It's a way of processing complex ideas, solving problems, or simply expressing our inner monologue. The quality of our thoughts and the way we engage in self-talk are influenced by our overall mental state, which, in turn, is closely tied to both, our lifestyle and the habits that we have come to develop over time.

Living a healthy lifestyle is crucial for maintaining a positive and clear thought process, even when thinking out loud. When we prioritize physical health through exercise and balanced nutrition, it not only benefits our bodies but also enhances cognitive function. Regular exercise, for example, has been shown to boost mood and cognitive performance. Moreover, emotional well-being, nurtured through practices like mindfulness and stress management, contributes to a healthier thought process. A calm and balanced mind is better equipped to engage in constructive self-talk. Developing healthy habits, such as maintaining a regular sleep schedule, practicing mindfulness, and fostering a growth-oriented mindset, can significantly influence the quality of our self-talk. When we engage in positive self-dialogue and approach challenges with a problem-solving attitude, we are more likely to find effective solutions and maintain a radiant smile even in the midst of difficulties. Engaging in verbalizing our thoughts becomes a valuable occasion for productive introspection and the resolution of issues, exemplifying the elegance of a cultivated thought process and one's inner state of wellness.

So, next time you find yourself talking to yourself, don't be alarmed; it's a natural part of the thought process. Thinking out loud can be helpful in clarifying one's thoughts and feelings, it's in fact not a sign of madness as believed by some social lifestyle. Turn on the release valve and let it flow, build a skyscraper of healthy habits, and let your self-talk word reflect a beautiful outward expression.

Tongue Sucking

In the realm of thought processes, tongue-sucking can be likened to a self-soothing mechanism, akin to a baby's thumb-sucking. Although it may seem harmless, it involves the mouth being slightly open with the tongue protruding, creating a relaxed seal around the inner lips. This behavior is widely perceived as a method for self-comfort, actively contributing to a sense of relaxation and effectively aiding in the reduction of stress.

Hold up, hold up, hold it right there!! What?

Let's try that again; how does it make you look?

Tongue sucking can make someone appear as if they are sucking on something hard, with the mouth partially open and the tongue poking out, forming a relaxed air seal around the inner lips.

Ha-ha, ha-ha, standing ovation!

Do you care to try?

"This part of the tongue-sucking phenomenon can be done in a conscious state of mind, but it gets more interesting when it is done in an uncontrolled state of consciousness." One may never be able to create a definition of them self and the way one looks when the facial tongue-sucking features are coupled with the facial contours formed when they are captivated by their thoughts.

It is not uncommon to witness someone seemingly in a trance-like state, sucking their tongue in a repetitive and uncontrolled manner. This phenomenon is referred to as "tongue-sucking," and it is a behavior that is often seen in people who are in an uncontrolled state of consciousness.

Tongue-sucking represents a form of self-soothing activity observed in individuals who enter a trance-like state. It manifests as a repetitive, subconscious behavior often witnessed in those experiencing a relaxed, daydreaming condition. This practice is believed to serve as a means for individuals to regulate their emotions and restore a sense of serenity.

While the precise cognitive underpinnings of this behavior remain somewhat enigmatic, some theories posit that it acts as a tension-release mechanism and a cognitive focal point. People may adopt this behavior as a means to momentarily escape from reality and enter a state of relaxation. It is thought that the act of sucking stimulates the brain, facilitating the transition into a more tranquil mental state.

It's crucial to emphasize that tongue sucking, while not detrimental, might not be aesthetically appealing in terms of facial characteristics. Nonetheless, it serves as a valuable tool for returning to a state of calm and emotional self-regulation. This innate practice can serve as a means of temporary escapism and mental relaxation. Yet, it's imperative to maintain awareness of this behavior, monitoring it for excessiveness, and seeking alternative methods to effectively manage stress and anxiety.

Captivated by Your Thoughts

The human mind is an incredible thing. It can be the source of profound creativity, passion, and progress, while also being the cause of our own destruction. We are masters of our own thoughts, and our thoughts can take us to places that we could never have imagined. We can be captivated by our own thoughts, and this can lead us into an uncontrolled state of consciousness. When we are captivated by our thoughts, it can manifest itself in many ways. We can become so focused on our thoughts that we forget what is happening, and we may start to drift away from reality. This can lead to an uncontrolled state of consciousness, where our thoughts take us to places that we never intended to go.

Our facial expressions can also reflect this state when we are caught in an uncontrolled state of consciousness. Our facial expressions may become slack and unresponsive, or our eyes may become wide and unfocused. This uncontrolled state of consciousness can be a dangerous thing, as it can lead us to make decisions that we would not normally make. It can also cause us to become isolated, as we are so focused on our own thoughts that we forget to interact with the active environment. Therefore, it is important to be aware of our thoughts and to be mindful of our facial expressions when we are in an uncontrolled state of consciousness. By becoming aware of our thoughts and paying attention to our facial expressions, we can begin to better manage our thoughts and emotions and maintain control of our state of consciousness. This will allow us in making a lot healthier and better decisions, eventually enjoying better relationships with people, too.

To maintain control of our thoughts and emotions, it is important to pay attention to our facial expressions and be mindful of what our thoughts are taking us to. We should take action to ensure that our thoughts and emotions do not lead us down a path of undesired display of facial expressions and other outward manifestations that could result in unwanted consequences.

Being captivated by your thoughts can be a fascinating state of consciousness where your mind takes center stage, guiding you through a journey of introspection, creativity, and contemplation. This uncontrolled state of consciousness, often experienced during moments of deep reflection or inspiration, can lead to insights and personal growth. It's during these moments that we can truly appreciate the interconnectedness of our inner world and the importance of living a healthy lifestyle and developing good habits.

Living a healthy lifestyle is one of the cornerstones of maintaining a clear and vibrant mental landscape. Regular exercise, balanced nutrition, and adequate sleep provide the physical foundation for a healthy thought process. A well-nourished body can foster a well-nourished mind, making it more receptive to refined thoughts and creative bursts of inspiration.

Cultivating constructive mental habits like mindfulness, self-reflection, and nurturing a growth-oriented mindset can substantially enhance the quality of your thoughts when they capture your attention. decrease word count just a bit.

When your thoughts captivate you, the outcome is particularly favorable when it manifests as a lovely outward expression, like a beaming smile. This smile serves as a mirror reflecting the delight and contentment stemming from embracing moments of insight and self-discovery. It effectively conveys the profound connection between inner wellness, a robust thought process, and the very essence of our consciousness. It stands as a powerful testament to the remarkable potency of holistic well-being, where physical health, mental vigor, and emotional equilibrium seamlessly converge, giving rise to moments of exceptional lucidity, profound wisdom, and boundless inspiration

.

CHAPTER 4

UNRAVELING THE COGNITIVE MYSTERY

There is a facial expression for almost every emotion that you feel. For example, there's a facial expression for laughter, sadness, and happiness, but these are things you do when you are conscious. You can make a choice to show happiness, sadness, fear, disgust, anger, contempt, or surprise. So, in fact, you are conscious and may be aware of how you may look and how people will interpret these facial gestures or facial expressions. The default face in very difficult, almost next to impossible to recreate when you are conscious of yourself, the contours are next to impossible to capture with a selfie or posing for a glamour shot, therefore a person in a lifetime might never get a chance to see their default face and what they really look like when they are captivated by their thoughts. Just saying, if your day of reckoning is anything like mine, it could be tough, mine was a laughing beauty to behold.

Cognitive Consciousness

Cognitive consciousness is a state of being that is often associated with human experience. It is the awareness of one's own thoughts, feelings, and actions. Cognitive consciousness can be a complex concept and is left for a lot of different theories and interpretations. It is the ability to think consciously. This involves being able to recognize and interpret thoughts, feelings, and actions. It is the capacity to reason, reflect, and make decisions. It is the foundation of our ability to learn and grow.

When we think consciously, our minds are actively engaged in problem-solving, decision-making, and forming opinions. We use our cognitive processes to make sense of the cosmos and to better understand ourselves. Hence, the awareness and functioning of our cognitive consciousness play a pivotal role in our mental and emotional wellness.

Cognitive consciousness is not a one-time event but rather an ongoing process. It is constantly evolving as we gain new experiences and knowledge.

"Through cognitive consciousness, we can challenge our own beliefs and assumptions and develop new perspectives."

Although it is a difficult concept to define, it is an essential part of the human experience. It is the foundation of our ability to think, reason, and reflect. It is our capacity to learn, grow, and form meaningful connections with others.

I do not claim to be a neuroscientist, but I have done some research on the brain, and in particular, the cerebral cortex and the limbic system, and my findings were astonishing.

There are five basic functions of the cerebral cortex, and it plays a key role in memory, attention perception, awareness thought language, and consciousness. This sheet of natural tissue has up to six layers of nerve cells. It is covered by many things and often referred to as gray matter; needless to say, I got a chuckle when I read that. Gray matter! I said to myself. It was my curiosity that drove me to persistently delve deeper, seeking additional information and a clearer understanding.

We often think of facial expressions as simple expressions of emotion, but they can tell us a lot about the inner workings of the mind. Our facial expressions are controlled by the cerebral cortex and limbic system, two significant components of the brain. The cerebral cortex is responsible for higher-level cognitive processes, while the limbic system is responsible for the regulation of emotion and memory.

The cerebral cortex is the largest part of the human brain and is responsible for many important functions, including thought processes and emotional facial expressions. It is divided into four lobes: the frontal, parietal, temporal, and occipital lobes. Each lobe is responsible for specific functions, such as memory, language, and problem-solving. The frontal lobe is the most important for thought processes, as it is responsible for the majority of higher-level thinking and decision-making.

The frontal lobe is also responsible for emotional expressions. This is because the frontal lobe is connected to the limbic system, which is responsible for managing emotions. The limbic system is composed of several structures, including the amygdala and hippocampus, both of which are involved in emotional regulation. The amygdala is responsible for detecting and responding to emotional signals, while the hippocampus is responsible for processing and storing memories.

The connection between the frontal lobe and the limbic system is important for understanding how the brain processes thought processes and emotional facial expressions. When the frontal lobe perceives a stimulus, such as a thought or an emotion, it sends a signal to the limbic system. The limbic system then processes the signal and sends a response back to the frontal lobe. This response can be an emotional facial expression, which can indicate how the person is feeling. Recent research has shown that the way in which these various brain regions interact with each other and with the body can have a significant impact on our thought process and facial expression. Specifically, the amygdala can exert an impact on our capacity to perceive and react to facial expressions, whereas the prefrontal cortex can wield influence over our capacity to manage and modulate our emotions.

The limbic system is a complex network of interconnected structures located within the brain responsible for regulating emotion, behavior, and memory. It is essential for our everyday functioning and is the source of our thoughts, feelings, and behavior. It plays an important role in our ability to learn and remember, and it is also the source of our emotional reactions. The limbic system is composed of several connected structures, including the amygdala, hippocampus, thalamus, hypothalamus, and cingulate gyrus. The amygdala is the structure most closely associated with emotional processing, and it is involved in the regulation of fear, aggression, and anxiety. The hippocampus is responsible for memory formation, while the thalamus is responsible for relaying sensory signals from the body to the brain. The hypothalamus is responsible for regulating homeostasis, and the cingulate gyrus is involved in the processing of emotions and sensations.

One of the primary functions of the limbic system is to process and regulate thoughts. Thoughts are the result of our conscious and unconscious mental processes, and the limbic system helps to regulate and organize them. It is thought to be responsible for zoning out and daydreaming, as well as other cognitive functions such as problem-solving, creativity, and decision-making. The limbic system is also responsible for regulating emotions and behaviors. It is thought to be the source of our feelings, such as happiness, anger, sadness, and fear. It is also responsible for the regulation of behavior, such as the ability to control our impulses and make decisions.

Overall, the limbic system is an integral part of our cognitive and emotional functioning and is responsible for regulating thoughts, emotions, and behaviors. It plays an important role in our daily functioning and is essential for our overall health and well-being. What was even more interesting from my research is that there are basically two distinct differences in the way facial expression is generated. They are classified as posed facial expressions and emotional facial expressions. I particularly want to take a closer look at these rather interesting facial expressions, as I research this, I learn that we can and also cannot control them due to the relationship and how they pass through the brain.

Posed Facial Expression

These expressions are consciously created traveling through our brain's cerebral cortex, which plays a role in thought, language, and consciousness. These are expressions that the sender intends to show. As it passes through our cortex, we have control over them; this is where display rules are managed.

Posed facial expressions are deliberate and conscious displays of emotions through one's facial features. These facial expressions are commonly utilized in social situations to convey distinct emotions or messages; however, they can also serve multiple alternative functions, including concealing genuine emotions or improving the effectiveness of communication.

Posed facial expressions are closely linked to our thoughts and emotions. Our thoughts and feelings trigger specific neural pathways in the brain, which then translate into facial expressions. For example, when we feel happy, our brain releases neurotransmitters like dopamine, which leads to the activation of facial muscles that create a smile. Conversely, when we feel anger or sadness, different neural circuits result in corresponding facial expressions like frowns or scowls. Your thoughts and emotions are the driving force behind the creation of posed facial expressions.

However, our ability to control posed facial expressions is a testament to the brain's remarkable capacity for cognitive control. The prefrontal cortex, a region associated with higher order thinking and decision-making, plays a crucial role in regulating facial expressions. This means that we can intentionally adjust or mask our true emotions by altering our facial expressions, a process known as emotional regulation. For example, during a job interview, someone may consciously control their facial expressions to appear confident and composed, even if they feel nervous. This ability to manipulate our facial expressions demonstrates the intricate connection between our thoughts, the brain, and our capacity for self-regulation. Additionally, it underscores the significance of social and situational factors in shaping our decisions to either reveal or mask our emotions through our facial expressions.

Emotional Facial Expression

These types of expressions are fed by innate emotional reactions to stimuli and do not pass through the cerebral cortex, leaving no time for consciousness or awareness. This can also lead to micro expressions, which are considered leakage of our true internal emotions before we have time to become aware of the emotion and possibly control it in one way or another.

More interesting is what I discovered about Micro Expressions. These Facial expressions can also show hidden feelings and thoughts. They appear without our permission or awareness, spontaneously and unconsciously. These involuntary facial expressions can occur in less than half a second. Due to the person not being aware they are displaying these expressions; it provides an insight into their true thoughts and emotions. Facial expressions can be powerful tools when it comes to communicating one's thoughts and feelings. They can be used to convey a wide range of emotions, from joy and excitement to anger and sadness. However, the way in which we express our emotions can vary depending on the situation. Our facial expressions have the capacity to be deliberately manipulated or coerced to convey a specific emotion, or they can adopt a more emotional nature, faithfully mirroring our authentic feelings.

Posed facial expressions are deliberate and can be used to manipulate how others perceive us. They can be used to make us appear more professional or confident or to hide our true feelings. This type of expression is often used in business settings when a person wants to appear in control and exude a certain level of confidence. It is more commonly employed in social settings by individuals seeking to appear at ease when they feel discomfort.

On the other hand, emotional facial expressions are more genuine and reflect our true feelings. These expressions are spontaneous and often take on an unconscious form. They can be used to convey a variety of emotions, including sadness, anger, surprise, and joy. Emotional expressions are typically more difficult to control and can be seen as more authentic than posed expressions. Our thought process can directly influence our facial expressions, particularly when we enter an uncontrolled state of consciousness, completely absorbed by our thoughts.

To what extent do your thoughts shape your identity? Does the adage "as a man thinks in his heart, so is he" extend to one's physical attributes?

"Thought is the act of thinking and the outcome of
a mental activity cogitation."

Thought is the past tense of the word think, which means to conceive in the mind example, deeply concentrating. The thought process   prompts an emotional response to what is on the mind at that time; this emotional response will cause a display in the physical realm; it's what I called the "three tier principle."

The Three-Tier Principle

Thoughts: what is on your mind causes you to enter into an uncontrolled state of consciousness. This is the moment when you are immersed in your thoughts, devoid of self-awareness.

Emotional response: This pertains to the reaction of your emotions to your thoughts.

Facial expression: This is a display in the physical realm. The facial contours make your face look a certain way during that instant of time. As soon as you come back to reality or become conscious of yourself and your surroundings, those facial contours immediately change. These are the facial contours that tell a person's story; these contours only show up based on a state of mind and will reflect a person thought, hence translating the aphorism, as a man thinks in his heart, "so he looks."

Our thoughts have immense power over our lives. They shape our actions, our words, and our character. When we think negative thoughts, we often feel negative emotions, and those emotions can affect how we act and how we are perceived by others. On the other hand, when we engage in positive thinking, we have the potential to cultivate positive emotions and project a positive outward demeanor.

It is important to recognize the power of our thoughts and to take steps to ensure that our thoughts are positive. One way to do this is to practice mindfulness. This involves being present and aware of our thoughts and feelings without judgment. With mindfulness, we can observe our thoughts and feelings without becoming entangled in them. This heightened awareness empowers us to choose our responses to life events. Earlier, we discussed life events as inputs to our thoughts; sometimes, a filter is needed to screen out unwanted sensory input.

"Life events are inputs to your thoughts. Filter well! because your thoughts are powerful enough to shape your character."
~~ Inspired ~~.

L. A. Chambers

Another way to use the power of our thoughts is to practice gratitude. Gratitude is the practice of focusing on the good things in life, regardless of our circumstances. When we are grateful, our hearts open and we become more aware of the abundance in our lives. This can have a positive effect on our character as we become more kind, compassionate, and patient with those we encounter.

We can use the power of our thoughts to create a positive outlook on life. When we focus on the positive aspects of our lives, we become more optimistic and resilient in the face of challenges. This helps us to stay focused and to stay motivated even when things are difficult. Our thoughts have incredible power. They can shape our emotions, our character, and our outward display. Becoming mindful of our thoughts, practicing gratitude, and maintaining a positive outlook, we can use the power of our thoughts to create a beautiful life for ourselves.

Intellectual Behavior

In simple terms, intellectual behavior is the idea that our thoughts and ideas influence our behavior. We all have a unique way of looking at the world, and our thoughts can shape our behavior. I believe that our thoughts can directly affect our behavior, either positively or negatively. For example, if someone is feeling anxious about a situation, their thoughts can cause them to become more anxious. The same is true if someone is feeling excited or hopeful about something. Our thoughts can also cause us to be more creative or to think more rationally.

It is important to understand that our thoughts are not the only thing that influences our behavior. Our environment, the people we surround ourselves with, and our experiences are inputs associated with circumstances of life events and can all shape our behavior. For instance, someone in a supportive and kind social circle is more likely to exhibit kindness and self-support. Likewise, exposure to a creativity-promoting environment tends to boost one's own creativity.

Intellectual behavior is an important aspect of our lives, as it helps us to make sense of the society that we live in. It is essential that we strive to think critically and objectively and to be open to different perspectives and ideas. This can help us to develop our own unique way of approaching the world and filter out unwanted events of life. While we can agree that we not always have control of all the things that happen to us throughout our life, we do have the power of choice, I urge you to choose well, you see, Life events, both significant and mundane, have the power to leave indelible imprints on our intellectual behavior. From childhood to adulthood, a myriad of experiences shapes the way we perceive the world, interpret information, and make decisions. These events could range from personal achievements, failures, traumas, relationships, cultural exposures, career advancements, to life-altering moments. Each encounter adds a layer of complexity to our intellectual makeup, molding our thoughts and influencing subsequent behaviors.

It's like a catalyst for cognitive growth, forcing us to confront new challenges and adapt our thinking patterns. Adversity, for instance, often serves as a powerful trigger for intellectual development. Overcoming challenges requires us to analyze the situation, think creatively, and find solutions. In doing so, we expand our cognitive capacities, enhancing our problem-solving skills and resilience. Life events push us to explore uncharted territories within our minds, fostering intellectual growth and development.

Think about it for a minute! Human beings possess a remarkable capacity for intellectual behavior, which encompasses our thoughts, cognitive processes, and decision-making abilities. Our intellectual behavior is influenced by a multitude of factors, including genetics, upbringing, education, and societal influences. One of the most profound impacts of life events is their ability to shift our perspectives, broadening our intellectual horizons. When we encounter diverse cultures, ideas, or belief systems, our preconceived notions and biases are challenged. Experiencing different worldviews can dismantle cognitive rigidity, promoting empathy, understanding, and intellectual flexibility. Does this enable us to approach situations with a broader outlook, enhance our critical thinking and problem-solving abilities? I think so.

Our intellectual behavior is a complex interplay of various factors, and life events occupy a central role in this intricate web. The experiences we encounter throughout our lives have the power to mold our thoughts, broaden our perspectives, and catalyze cognitive growth.

In this context, intellectual behavior reflects the cognitive processes that underlie our capacity for critical thinking, problem-solving, and knowledge acquisition. It encompasses a range of mental activities, from logical reasoning and analytical thinking to creativity and intellectual curiosity. Living a healthy lifestyle and cultivating healthy habits are essential factors that contribute to an optimal cognitive process, ultimately leading to a beautiful outward expression especially that radiant smile that signifies intellectual fulfillment.

A healthy lifestyle and good social habits play a pivotal role in supporting cognitive health. Regular exercise, for instance, enhances blood flow to the brain, proper nutrition, rich in antioxidants and nutrients, provides the brain with the resources it needs for optimal performance. Sufficient sleep is equally critical, as it allows the brain to consolidate information, process emotions, and prepare for a new day of intellectual challenges.

In general term "healthy habits," could be interpreted with more emphasis and differently by different people, but nevertheless, healthy habits such as continuous learning, mindfulness, and the pursuit of intellectual passions, are integral to fostering a healthy thought process. Engaging in lifelong learning keeps the mind active and adaptable, promoting intellectual growth and preventing cognitive decline. Mindfulness practices, like meditation, enhance focus and concentration, allowing for clearer, more deliberate thinking. Engaging in intellectual hobbies not only activates the mind but also generates joy and satisfaction, often resulting in a radiant smile. It undoubtedly contributes to intellectual fulfillment.

It is intricately connected to the cognitive processes that shape our thinking and problem-solving abilities. To nurture a healthy thought process that results in a radiant smile, it is crucial to prioritize a healthy lifestyle and cultivate good habits that support cognitive well-being. When our minds are vibrant and our intellectual pursuits are fueled by curiosity and enthusiasm, the result is a radiant smile that signifies positive intellectual behavior, a direct translation of fulfillment and contentment.

CHAPTER 5

SPHERE OF EMOTIONAL INFLUENCE

The Unseen Face

If you know what you look like when you are not looking at yourself when you are captivated by thoughts, you might never want to be seen looking like that ever!!!

The thing about this concept is that you might never see what your default face looks like until a photo is taken or it just got caught on tape. You can become aware of how you look if someone is honest and open enough to tell you.

I was made aware of my default face just by being present in a technical training session; for a few minutes, I went off into deep thoughts about events that were on my mind and needed to be resolved; by the time I came back to reality the entire table directly across from me was totally distracted by my default face. Some resorted to whispering, some had silly grins, and some had the balls to tell me what I looked like. For those "little rascals" who had the balls to tell me, today I am forever grateful. I immediately became conscious of my distracting default face.

My problem was "sucking my tongue," and that, coupled with those fascial contours created when I started to gaze into space, and totally captivated by my thoughts, left my appearance much to be desired. I became cognizant of my distracting default face and is now super conscious of it and try never to be caught looking like that again, and I mean "ever"!! Never to be caught looking like that again, "ever"!!

"My will, resilience, and determination to change my default face, was flipped into all-wheel drive and turbo charged mode."

"You are your thoughts, and your thoughts are you."
~~ Inspired ~~.

L. A. Chambers

Because of this reality, I find myself becoming an expert of spotting default face, it's like I have developed a professional skillset, an ability driven by cognizance and volition to do something about improving my outward expression.

My developed ability to spot default face is so learned, I can spot those curios gaze aligned with those special facial contours with ease, I can't help myself but to see it almost every time I am in a meeting, in a presentation, when people are not distracted, when people are by them self, using their computer, doodling, or just talking to themselves. I decided to write this book and be the "Johnny-on-the-spot" that helps someone to become conscious of how they might look when they are captivated by their thoughts. The contours that form your facial expression when your thoughts take you into an uncontrolled state of consciousness, by default, make your face look a certain way at that instance in time.

As soon as you come back to reality or "come back to earth" and become conscious of yourself and your surroundings, those contours immediately change, and your face is now showing an expression of a new emotional response, in alignment with the present environment's influence, for example, laughing, crying, excitement and just about any other vibe present.

These facial Contours that form the default face when you enter an uncontrolled state of consciousness, totally captivated by your thoughts are the emphasis, it's my "WHY."

These facial contours are like chapters in a person's life story, uniquely revealing themselves based on one's state of mind and ultimately reflecting their thoughts. This lends profound significance to the translated aphorism, "as a man thinks in his heart, so is he," or as it can be aptly put, "so he looks."

From my observation people with bad experience from broken relationships, fall out at work, been accused, treated unfairly, told lies about, got the thumbs down on social media and so on, often develop different facial expression that is easily seen by others, but is almost impossible to recreate in a conscious state of mind, therefore a person may never get seen their default face.

Prolonged stimuli create hurting people; hurting people go to bed thinking about it, wake up thinking about it, and go to work thinking about it; these thoughts start to form the wrinkles in your face, the shape of the lips, eyes, cheek, and facial muscles. "By default," meaning when you are not looking at yourself when you enter an uncontrolled state of consciousness, and are captivated by your thoughts, your face by default takes this shape.

So, does your thoughts really define you?

Is the condition of your heart set up to enable the flow of pure and radiant thoughts, to yield a beautiful outward expression?

Our thoughts have immense power over our lives. They shape our actions, our words, and our character. When we think negative thoughts, we often feel negative emotions, and those emotions can affect how we act and how we are perceived by others. Conversely, when we think positive thoughts, we can create positive emotions and a positive outward character display.

In earlier chapters of this book, we spoke about "life events" and how they form inputs to our thoughts. Sometimes, we need a filter to keep out unwanted events of life that enter our thoughts through our five senses.

It is important to recognize the power of our thoughts and to take steps to ensure that our thoughts are positive. One way to do this is to practice mindfulness, in simple terms, this is the quality or state of being conscious or aware of something.

"Life events are inputs to your thoughts; filter well, because your thoughts are powerful enough to shape your character."
~~ Inspired ~~.

L. A. Chambers

Mindfulness involves being present and aware of our thoughts and feelings without judgment. When we become mindful, we can observe our thoughts and feelings without getting caught up in them. This allows us to be more aware of our inner state and to choose our reactions to the events in our lives.

Our thoughts have incredible power. They can shape our emotions, our character, and our outward display. If we become mindful of our thoughts, practice gratitude, and maintain a positive outlook, we can use the power of our thoughts to create a beautiful life for ourselves.

"Our thoughts indeed play a significant role in defining who we are, shaping our beliefs, values, and our overall identity."

These inner musings influence our emotional state, our decision-making processes, and even our outward expression, including the way our face looks when we are in an uncontrolled state of consciousness. Our cognitive processes are at the heart of this intricate relationship between our thoughts and our outward appearance. The thoughts that we harbor deep within our hearts often manifest on our faces, particularly when we're in uncontrolled states of consciousness. In moments of joy, our faces light up with smiles, radiating the positivity we feel within.

On the other hand, during times of distress or anger, our facial expressions can become tense and furrowed, mirroring the turmoil that is within. This connection between our inner thoughts and outward expression, especially those that show up on our face, is a living testament to the influence of our cognitive processes on our physical demeanor.

The cognitive process itself plays a pivotal role in this dynamic. The thoughts we generate are influenced by our perceptions, past experiences, and belief systems.

Our minds continuously analyze and interpret the events of life that pass through our filter, shaping our emotional responses and the way we express them. Cultivating self-awareness and emotional intelligence allows us to understand the impact of our thoughts on our outward expression. With practice and determination, we can learn to manage our thoughts and emotions more effectively, leading to a more controlled and intentional external demeanor.

Our thoughts constitute the foundational elements of our identity, inevitably exerting their influence on our outward expressions, encompassing our appearance when we find ourselves in an uncontrolled state of consciousness.

The ancient wisdom captured in the aphorism, "As a man thinketh in his heart, so is he," emphasizes the profound connection between our thoughts and our identity."

Our thoughts are the architects of our inner world, shaping our values, beliefs, and emotions, which, in turn, define who we are as individuals. This interplay between our innermost thoughts and our outward appearance, particularly when we are in an uncontrolled state of consciousness and captivated by our thoughts, reveals the intricate nature of the cognitive process.

When we are immersed in our thoughts, whether through deep reflection, creativity, or introspection, our faces often serve as windows into our inner selves. Our expressions can mirror the emotions and mental states we experience at that moment.

"A radiant smile during a moment of inspiration or a furrowed brow when grappling with a complex problem reflects the emotional resonance of our thoughts."

These uncontrolled expressions are a testament to the potent influence of our cognitive processes on our outward appearance. The cognitive process itself is a dynamic force that guides our thoughts, emotions, and actions. It involves the way our minds perceive, interpret, and respond to the environmental influence. As our thoughts ebb and flow, driven by our innermost convictions and subconscious processes, the contours of our face respond accordingly, forming a face that you might never get to see. If we are able to Develop mindfulness and emotional intelligence, it can help us become more attuned to this connection, allowing us to navigate our thoughts and emotions with greater awareness. Fostering a positive thought process and nurturing our inner well-being, we can cultivate a radiant outward expression that reflects our authenticity and emotional harmony, even in moments when we are captivated by our thoughts.

Building a Tower of Memories

Emotions are broadly classified into two categories: primary and secondary. Primary emotions are universally innate, while secondary emotions are learned reactions to specific triggers. These fundamental feelings, like joy, sorrow, anger, fear, love, and hate, are universally shared by people, regardless of their cultural or background differences. Secondary emotions are more complex and nuanced. These include jealousy, envy, guilt, shame, pride, and embarrassment. Secondary emotions are often the result of socialization and individual experiences. Let's face it, these are unique words used to identify a person's emotion but can have similar physical manifestations and instinctive behavior.

It is important to note that emotions can be both positive and negative. Positive emotions can be described as pleasurable, such as joy, contentment, and love. Negative emotions can be described as uncomfortable, such as anger, fear, and sadness.

The thing about it is that the effects of our thoughts in the physical realm gets more pronounced with age; things like bitterness, unforgiveness, unresolved issues, broken relationships and other stressful situations have a way of adding up and becoming festered as you get older. It's like "building a skyscraper of habits." This is not where it ends. Through the perpetuation of emotional habits, you are essentially and unwittingly constructing a tower of enduring memories. Think about it, if you are building a tower of memories, you should build one that can help you survive emotional turbulence, filter out negativity, and set you up for success. Be sure to fill your emotional hard drive with positivity, healthy thoughts, and fond memories, it's building a solid foundation that will stand the test.

"Build a tower of memories that will withstand emotional turbulence and dissipate seismically induced events of life."
~~ Inspired ~~.

L. A. Chambers

Some people keep a journal. They journal all the bad things that happen to them. Some read it every day, and this means they will never heal. The more time you spend in "thought mode," the more time you allocate to the growth and formation of the muscles that sculpt the contours of your default face.

People who keep a journal of happy moments in their lives may find that reading these entries daily can profoundly influence their perspective, habits, and overall disposition.

Self-awareness

The good thing about a default face is that it can be adjusted. If you become cognizant of it, then you can take actions to improve it. Being aware of your default face is one of the first steps of taking action to making it work in your favor. Normally when a person is caught in an uncontrolled state of consciousness, for example, daydreaming, people will ask something like, "What are you thinking about now?" The typical response is: "Nothing!"

But the fact is that they are, do you know what you look like at that moment when you are captivated by your thoughts, what you are thinking about has totally captured your self-awareness; this could be considered a mild state of "stupor," and you are now looking just the way you are thinking.

Do your thoughts make you angry and sad or happy and joyful? Is your default face a *"pretty face"* decorated with unhappy memories, un-forgiveness, broken promises, betrayal, and unfavorable treatment at work and home? As you grow older these facial decorations get more polished and pronounced, highlighting the buildup matter inside you.

It's shaping your default face, you are now becoming and looking like a direct replica of your thoughts.

So, do your thoughts really define you?

Speaking of self-awareness, how about self-exploration? The idea of continuous self-searching and the act of applying the filter to events that are input to our thoughts and emotions.

I believe the journey to discovering your true inner self requires a commitment to self-exploration and, more importantly, self-acceptance. It is a process of understanding yourself on a deep level and exploring those things that are unique to you; these include your beliefs, values, feelings, and behaviors. With an increased self-awareness, you can gradually discern the patterns, habits, and behaviors that have ceased to be beneficial, allowing you to consciously identify the thoughts and beliefs that contribute to your inner peace.

Self-discovery begins with you and your will to take action to gain understanding and clarity. It is important to be honest with yourself about your strengths, weaknesses, and motivations.

Be aware of the things that bring you joy, as well as the things that cause you distress. The more aware you are of yourself and the inputs to your thoughts, the better you will be able to identify your core values and beliefs, understand why you react in certain ways, what motivates your behavior especially in hurtful situations. Responding to the hurting stimuli requires a great deal of emotional horsepower and can consume a person and the thought process. When you are consumed by a hurting stimulus, it affects one's ability to think rationally and make healthy choices. Most of their time is spent thinking about the circumstances and not about their own well-being.

When you are hurting, naturally, your human characteristics form an emotional response, whether it is good or bad, whether you are conscious of it or not. If you are truly honest with yourself, you would reveal it. However, a person might not be aware or cognizant of the hurting stimuli because it could be the accepted way of life or environmental norms that are practiced form day to day.

One relationship between emotions and the thought process can be understood by looking at how emotions can affect the way we think. Emotions can influence our thought processes by increasing or decreasing our level of alertness, our attention span, and our ability to reason. It can also affect our memory and our ability to recall information.

When we feel a strong emotion, it can have an immediate impact on our thought process. We may be more likely to act impulsively and make decisions based on our emotional state. We may also be more likely to make decisions that are not rational or well thought out increasing the chances to make mistakes.

"When we are in an uncontrolled state of consciousness, our emotions can become stronger and more difficult to manage."

It often manifests with physical characteristics that others see, but you don't. In addition, it can lead to irrational decisions that may have serious consequences. For example, a person may be more likely to make a risky financial decision and have undesirable behavioral display when they are feeling anxious or angry. This can be particularly detrimental when someone is conscious but struggles to manage their emotions.

It is important to be aware of the potential for our emotions to influence our thought processes. We should strive to become more mindful of our emotional states and work to manage our emotions. Let's endeavor to do this, set ourselves up for success, this way we can ensure that our thoughts and decisions are rational and well thought out, even when we are feeling intense emotions.

Hurt can evoke an emotional response. Sometimes it can turn to violent reactions, aggressive word exchange, silence, tears, or even emotional concealment. It can also lead to malice, parting of relationship, living with un-forgiveness, or, as some would say, I forgive, but I do not forget, keeping then in lingering hurt mode.

Make no mistake! But this is when it rains in your face, all the time you spend thinking about how this could happen to me, what bad thing I would like to do to that brute, or how I wish they broke a leg. This is what I would refer to as "building up invisible energy," and all these invisible energies are constantly "pumping emotional steroids" into your facial formation and perspicaciously opposing your "smile testosterone." Self-awareness is a crucial element in understanding how our thoughts define who we are. It involves recognizing and acknowledging our emotions, thoughts, and their impact on our behavior and well-being. When we cultivate self-awareness, we gain insight into the intricate relationship between our inner world and our outward expressions, including our smiles. Nonetheless, emotional pain, harbored resentment, and unaddressed negative life situations can disrupt this intricate equilibrium, subsequently impacting our emotional responses and impeding our capacity to nurture positive thoughts and display beautiful outward expressions.

Emotional hurt, whether stemming from past traumas, conflicts, or negative experiences, can deeply influence our thought patterns and emotional well-being. These hurts can fester beneath the surface, coloring our perceptions and attitudes, and making it difficult to foster positive thoughts or maintain a radiant smile. The emotional reactions evoked by lingering, unresolved pain, emotional distress, and acts of unkindness have the potential to cast shadows over moments of joy and positivity, erecting a formidable barrier to authentic self-awareness.

Unforgiveness can further compound these issues. Holding onto grudges and refusing to forgive can perpetuate negative thought patterns and emotional distress. It keeps us tethered to the past and prevents us from moving forward with a lighter heart and a more positive outlook. The emotional burden of unforgiveness can cast a shadow upon our smiles, rendering it arduous to authentically convey feelings of joy or warmth in our interactions with others.

To address these challenges and regain our ability to develop good thoughts and express them with a genuine smile, it's essential to cultivate self-awareness and engage in healing practices. Recognizing and acknowledging our emotional hurt and unforgiveness is the first step towards healing. Seeking support through therapy or counseling can provide valuable tools to process these emotions and work towards forgiveness and emotional restoration.

As we release the burdens of hurt and resentment, we create space for positive thoughts and the radiant smiles that come with true self-awareness and emotional healing. Emotional healing is a transformative journey that involves confronting, processing, and ultimately releasing emotional wounds and baggage. It is intimately connected to changing our thought processes and creating beautiful outward expressions, particularly on our face. As we heal emotionally, we free ourselves from the burdens of negative emotions, past traumas, and unresolved conflicts. This emerging emotional liberation empowers us to nurture more beneficial thought patterns, which in turn cultivates a greater sense of positivity, resilience, and self-compassion. As a result of this inner transformation, our countenances gradually start to mirror the authenticity, serenity, and joy that we experience within.

Emotional healing not only improves our own well-being but also enhances our interactions with others, as our beautiful outward expressions become a source of inspiration and connection for those we encounter.

Emotional healing is akin to polishing a gem; it unveils our inner beauty and radiance. As we release the emotional scars that may have clouded our thoughts and expressions, we make room for self-love, self-acceptance, and a greater sense of inner peace. This transformation doesn't just impact our faces; it transcends into every facet of our lives. We become more open, empathetic, and able to connect with others on a deeper level, fostering a harmonious environment where beautiful outward expressions of kindness, understanding, and joy become the norm.

As we release the emotional scars that may have clouded our thoughts and expressions, we make room for self-love, which is a game changing and transformative journey towards acceptance and compassion for ourselves. Emotional scars, often stemming from past hurts, trauma, or negative experiences, can create a barrier between us and self-love. These emotional scars may surface as self-doubt, self-criticism, or an enduring feeling of unworthiness, casting a shadow over our capacity to wholeheartedly and truly accept ourselves for who we are.

Practicing self-love begins with recognizing our inherent worth and acknowledging that we deserve kindness, care, and forgiveness, just like everyone else. The path to healing emotional scars starts with self-awareness, where we accept the pain's impact on how we perceive ourselves. Through therapeutic methods, self-reflection, and the practice of mindfulness, we initiate the gradual journey of emotional recovery.

As we undertake the path of self-healing and self-love, our thought patterns undergo a transformation. We shift from self-critique to self-compassion, from negative self-talk to affirmations of self-worth, and from self-judgment to accepting our imperfections. These positive mental changes foster an inner environment that promotes a sense of peace and balance, and as a result, our outward expressions undergo a transformation.

Our faces become a canvas that reflects this newfound self-love. A warm and genuine smile emerges, mirroring the love and acceptance we've cultivated within ourselves. It's a smile that radiates not only beauty but also an inner peace and contentment that are truly transformative. Moreover, this beautiful outward expression of self-love extends beyond us, creating a ripple effect of positivity in our interactions with others, inspiring them to embark on their own journeys of self-acceptance and love.

Fuel the Smile Testosterone

What if you could fuel your smile with something that doesn't involve a physical object or a materialistic item? What if you could fill your smile with something that would last forever?

"Smile testosterone are fuel by happy thoughts, fond memories and healthy habits."
~~ Inspired ~~.

L. A. Chambers

Fuel the smile testosterone by building a tower of great memories and healthy habits, practice the act of taking time out of your day to do something that makes you happy. It could be as simple as taking a walk in the park, watching a movie, or spending time with your friends. Whatever it is that makes you feel good, that's what you should be focusing on. When you fuel your smile, you're taking the time to do something that brings you a sense of joy or satisfaction.

The great thing about this concept of fueling your smile is that it doesn't have to cost you anything. You don't necessarily need money or material possessions to make yourself feel better.

You can simply take the time to do something that you enjoy, whether it's reading a book, listening to music, or doing something creative. When you take the time to fuel your smile, you're taking a positive step toward improving your overall well-being. Think of it as an investment to build emotional resilience in those future challenging moments, give yourself a reason to smile, and add more joy to your life.

Take a minute to talk to somebody you realize is in an uncontrolled state of consciousness, captivated by their thought, and totally un-aware of their "make up face" and I am not talking about cosmetics. I am talking about push out lips, drop cheekbones and a wrinkled forehead. You could be the angelic presence that touches somebody's life, making them cognizant and poised to initiate a positive change.

We often hear it said that "actions speak louder than words," and that may be true, but the truth is that our thoughts can be just as revealing of our true selves and characters.

Our thoughts can tell us a lot about ourselves, our values, and our beliefs. They can show us what we really care about and what is important to us. They can significantly influence how we make decisions, shape our thoughts about the future, and approach all the challenges that life sends towards us.

As much as we all have the same nouns that identify our emotions, the inputs of our thoughts may differ because our personal exposure to life events may not be the same. What we allow to pass through our filter can impact our thoughts and reveal our innermost feelings and emotions. They can show us what we are really feeling, even if we don't necessarily want to admit it. They can also show us how we feel about ourselves and can help us to understand and accept our true selves.

Our thoughts also have the power to shape our reality. They can affect our outlook on life and how we approach different situations. They can lead us to make different choices and can help us to create a more positive future. The truth is that our thoughts reflect our true selves and our characters.

They can tell us a lot about who we are and help us be the best version of ourselves. So, it is important to take some time to reflect on our thoughts and to be mindful of what we are thinking; take a moment to smile and let it radiates from a pure heart.

CHAPTER 6

TELLING YOUR STORY

In reality, a person can use clothing to cover the body and enhance their persona with designer brands, but the face is frequently left exposed. This is the part that tells your story when you are in an uncontrolled state of consciousness and totally captivated by your thoughts.

"Your persona in this state is an aspect of your true self that
is presented to or perceived by others. Believe me,
you can display your "true colors" in an environment
where you would rather not."

I had a moment of truth in a training session and became the "laughingstock," I saw my colleague trying to tell my story on his face, which amplified the room with a big outburst of laughs; even I had to laugh at myself. With that re-enactment, I guess my emotional response to my thoughts did reveal a beautiful story of what was captivating me, the events of life that were inputs to my thoughts at that time needed a make-over. We all have a story to tell, and our thoughts can often be the best place to start. Our thoughts are deeply intertwined with our emotions and behaviors and can tell us a lot about our inner selves.

When we are happy and content, our thoughts will be positive, and our emotions and behavior will be reflective of that. On the other hand, when we are feeling anxious or stressed, our thoughts will typically be negative, and our emotions and behavior will follow suit, revealing our core values, beliefs, and preferences. When we think about what is important to us, what we stand for, and what we want to achieve, we form our true inner selves. These thoughts can then manifest themselves in our emotions and behavior in the form of intentional or unintentional actions or habits. The human mind is a powerful tool, capable of creating and perceiving stories that tell us a lot about who we are and how we view the world. Our thoughts are the windows into our innermost selves, reflecting our beliefs, feelings, and values in a way that no other medium can. Through our thoughts, we can tell our own story and gain insight into our true inner selves.

If we are able to maintain a positive mental attitude, it could help us to shape our experiences and beliefs positively, leading to better decision-making, a healthier outlook on life, reflecting our values and goals, and helping us make decisions that align with our core beliefs. By becoming aware of our thoughts, we can gain insight into our values, goals, and the kind of person we want to be. Life events that are input into our thoughts and can have a great influence on how we respond to various situations. Do we react to difficult situations with fear and anxiety or stay calm and focused on finding a solution? Do we become discouraged when things don't go our way, or do we keep pushing forward? Suppose we become cognizant of the inputs to our thoughts. In that case, it can provide insight into our emotional responses to different situations.

It can help us better understand how we can work to improve our reactions. How we respond to circumstances we face, especially the hurt stimuli, can manifest certain behaviors that say a thing or two about the character formed through our thoughts.

Our thoughts can be a powerful tool in understanding ourselves and our true inner selves. Let's pay attention, become aware of ourselves, and be cognizant of those inputs into our thoughts; we become mindful of how they affect our emotions and behavior to help us gain insight into our values, beliefs, preferences, and reactions. Let's gain a better understanding of ourselves, develop the volition to act, and create a positive change.

Ultimately, our thoughts can tell us a lot about our true-life story. Reflecting on our thoughts, we can gain valuable insight into our deepest feelings and motivations and use this knowledge to make our story beautiful. We can work on developing positive thinking patterns and using our thoughts to create a positive reality. We can harness the power of our thoughts to craft a narrative for our lives that is not only empowering and uplifting but also capable of making our personal story beautiful.

We all have a story, though oftentimes we can't articulate it, but your face will. The face you don't know will reflect an emotional response to your thoughts; these thoughts are made up of your experiences and events in life to which you are exposed.

If you are caught daydreaming or zoned out and captivated by your thoughts, others will see your default face; you are now looking like a replica of your thoughts. What are you thinking about? What kind of thoughts captivate you? are they reflecting a beautiful story? Are they thoughts of revenge, payback, doubt, love, excitement, and creativity? Take a moment to refocus, as we may not always find the words to describe how we are feeling, yet our thoughts and behavior silently narrate the story of who we are and everything that we have endured.

Our thoughts can often be a window into our innermost selves, revealing our deepest hopes, fears, and worries. It can tell us a lot about our emotional state, and the story they tell can be an important part of our personal growth and development. For example, suppose we find ourselves constantly worrying or ruminating on negative thoughts. In that case, it can be a sign that we need to work on managing our anxiety, not hold a grudge, forgive, and find creative ways to improve our mental health.

The things in life that build our experiences and influence our thoughts can also tell us a lot about our values and beliefs. If we find ourselves constantly questioning our decisions or choices, it can be a sign that we need to take a closer look at our values and how they're guiding our decisions. Similarly, if we find ourselves constantly seeking approval from others, it can be a sign that we need to work on boosting our self-confidence and developing our own sense of self-worth.

"Let's use our thoughts to shape our story
in a positive way."

If we focus on the good things in our lives, they can become a source of strength and resilience. Similarly, let's take the time to recognize our successes and accomplishments. We can start to build a sense of pride and self-confidence.

Recall that eureka moment? It gives you wings.

You may not be the person who impulsively jumps out of a bathtub and sprints down the street undressed, shouting, "I found it," but your face will undoubtedly express gratitude.

"Suppose you are caught in an uncontrolled state of consciousness, captivated by thoughts of success, creativity, beauty, and loveliness. In that case, I believe your default face will be the delight of a beautiful story."

Ultimately, the story our thoughts tell is up to us. We can choose to focus on the positive or the negative, and we can choose to create a beautiful and meaningful story. By cultivating positivity and gratitude, we can create a story reflecting our true inner self and emotional well-being.

"We all carry stories that may never be told,
stories written on our faces."

Our thoughts and emotions can be in constant flux and often leave a lasting impression on our faces. In an uncontrolled state of consciousness, our faces can vividly tell a story of a life that is rarely, if ever, seen or understood by others.

When we are in an uncontrolled state of consciousness, our faces may tell stories of fear, anger, pain, and sadness. Our faces may be contorted in ways that express the inner turmoil that we feel in that moment. Our eyes may be filled with tears, our eyes may be wide with terror, and our mouths may be pursed in anger or frustration. These expressions are a direct result of how we feel in that moment, and they tell the world exactly how we feel. Our faces can also tell stories of joy, courage, and hope in moments of uncontrolled consciousness. When we experience a moment of joy, our faces may break into wide smiles that convey the happiness we feel. When we feel courageous, our faces may convey an expression of strength and determination. When we are filled with hope, our faces may be lit up with a sense of optimism.

No matter what emotion we may be feeling in a moment of uncontrolled consciousness, our faces will always tell our story. Our faces will always show the world how we feel and think.

"Is your displayed story beautiful? Or is your story a beautiful story decorated with things like malice, un-forgiveness, doubt, and other hurtful experiences?"

Indeed, our face serves as an open book that tells the story of our inner world, with our thoughts being the driving force behind the narrative. A happy face reflects a story of healthy thoughts, brimming with positivity, joy, and contentment. It's a testament to a mind at ease, free from the weight of negativity, and radiates warmth and approachability, inviting positive interactions and connections with others.

On the other hand, a hurtful face narrates a story of inner turmoil, carrying the heavy burden of negative thoughts, emotional pain, or unresolved trauma. The furrowed brows, downturned lips, and tense expressions communicate the distress within, often creating barriers to authentic communication and connection. Such expressions are a call for empathy and understanding, signaling the need for healing and support.

Our faces, like mirrors, reflect the ongoing dialogue between our thoughts and emotions. They provide glimpses into our experiences, struggles, and triumphs, offering those around us insights into our inner narratives. By cultivating self-awareness and nurturing positive thought patterns, we can actively shape the story our face tells, allowing it to become a more authentic and radiant reflection of our inner selves. This process not only enriches our own well-being but also enhances our ability to connect with and understand the stories conveyed by the faces of those we encounter in our daily lives.

When our consciousness is primarily filled with positive thoughts and emotions, our faces light up with smiles that narrate tales of happiness, confidence, and inner peace. These expressions are not just aesthetically pleasing but also possess an almost magnetic quality, drawing others into our positive aura and nurturing a deeper sense of connection.

> "A joyful face is like a beacon, inviting joy and positivity into our interactions with others."

> "Our faces are storytellers, painting vivid pictures of our inner world's ongoing narrative."

By nurturing an awareness of the intricate interplay between our thoughts and emotions, we acquire profound insights into our own mental and emotional conditions, granting us the ability to deliberately mold the narratives etched on our faces. This heightened level of self-awareness not only significantly elevates our emotional well-being but also profoundly bolsters our capacity to connect with and empathetically interpret the stories subtly woven into the expressions of the individuals we encounter, consequently nurturing more profound and authentically meaningful connections with others.

Make Your Story Beautiful with Love

Love is an emotion that has a profound effect on the human thought process. It has been said that love is the greatest emotion of all. It certainly has the power to influence our thoughts and feelings. When we are in a state of uncontrolled consciousness, love can make us display beautiful characters and facial expressions. This is because love is associated with a sense of joy, peace, and satisfaction. We often find ourselves smiling, laughing, and being open to the views of others without the need for discrimination and judgement. Love makes us feel connected to the people we care about and can bring out the best in us. On the other hand, lack of love can also have a negative effect on our thought process. We may be irritable, anxious, and less likely to be open to interacting with others. We may be less likely to think of others and more likely to be focused on our own needs.

However, when it's all said and done, love has the power to inspire us and bring out the best in us. It can open us up to the beauty that exists in our society, in our homes and our active environment. It can make us feel connected to the people we care about and help us be more compassionate and understanding. Love is a powerful emotion, and it can have a profound effect on our thought process. Whether we are in a state of uncontrolled consciousness or not, it is important to remember that love can bring out the best in us and help us to be the best version of ourselves. We all have a story to tell, make your story beautiful and outstanding with love.

Here are a few tips.

Show yourself, love. Before we can truly love others, we must learn to love ourselves. Take time to do things that make you feel good and that bring you joy. Love yourself unconditionally, and don't be too hard on yourself when things don't go as planned.

Express your love to others. Show your family, friends, and partners how much you care. Make sure they know you appreciate them and value their efforts. Send them cards, compliment them, ensuring they know you're thinking of them.

Take time to do things you love. Spend time doing activities that bring you happiness, such as reading, painting, or playing a sport. Make sure to schedule time for these activities so that you can look forward to them and make the most of them.

Show kindness to others. Let people in your life know that you care for them and are thinking of them. Show kindness to strangers as well and be sure to spread positive vibes wherever you go. Have compassion for yourself and others. We all make mistakes and have our own struggles. Be understanding and compassionate of yourself and others. Show empathy and be willing to forgive both yourself and others. At the end of the day, the most important thing is to find joy in the journey and make it a meaningful one.

Make Your Story Beautiful with Gratitude

A person's life story is not just about the events that have taken place; it is also about how those events are remembered, how they impact the thought process, and how the person has grown from them. We can help to make our story beautiful by practicing gratitude. It is the recognition and appreciation of the good that exists in our lives. It is the practice of recognizing the positive aspects of life, even during difficult times. We can look back and appreciate the experiences that have shaped us.

We can acknowledge moments of joy and success and be thankful for them. We can also recognize the lessons that have been learned from difficult times and be grateful for the strength and resilience they have provided. I believe gratitude also brings us a sense of peace and contentment that will look good on a default face. It helps us to focus on what is good in our lives and to be thankful for the things that we have and allows us to look at our life with a sense of wonder and appreciation. it will help us to recognize the beauty in the ordinary, allows us to see the small moments of joy in our day-to-day lives that may otherwise go unnoticed, and enables us to appreciate the beauty existing in the little things and to find joy in the simple pleasures of life.

Reflecting on our life journey, we can rediscover the beauty within moments that might have otherwise faded into obscurity. We can discover joy in the little things and be genuinely thankful for the experiences that have molded us. The practice of gratitude can profoundly assist us in recognizing and cherishing the inherent beauty within our life story, even during the most challenging of times.

Here are a few tips:

Make gratitude a daily practice. Make a commitment to spend some time each day being mindful of the things you are grateful for in your life. This could be something as simple as taking a few moments to appreciate the sunshine coming through your window or taking a few extra minutes to savor a delicious meal. When you establish gratitude as a daily practice, you will discover that you'll progressively become attuned to and appreciate more of the good things in your life for which you can be thankful.

Find ways to express your gratitude. Whether it's writing, thank you notes, sending flowers, or taking the time to call or text someone to let them know how much they mean to you, expressing gratitude is an essential part of creating a beautiful story, you will most likely be remembered for it.

Take the time to appreciate yourself. Self-care is important in cultivating gratitude, so take the time to do things that make you feel good and give you energy. This can be as simple as taking a few minutes to relax in a hot bath or going for a walk-in nature.

When we take time to care for ourselves, we have more energy and appreciation for the good things in our lives. Creating a beautiful life story with gratitude is an investment in ourselves and our lives. When we invest in ourselves, we are investing in a life of abundance and joy.

As our thoughts gravitate towards gratitude, our outward expressions follow suit. Our faces light up with genuine smiles that convey the joy and appreciation we feel. These smiles are not forced or insincere; they are the natural byproduct of a heart filled with gratitude. They radiate warmth, approachability, and an inner contentment that is contagious. In turn, they inspire positivity and connection in our interactions with others.

Gratitude has the remarkable ability to infuse our life story with beauty and positivity, closely tied to how our thoughts shape our outward expressions.

As we cultivate a grateful mindset, our thoughts naturally align with the abundance and blessings that surround us on a daily basis. Instead of fixating on our limitations or challenges, we consciously and deliberately shift our focus to the numerous reasons we have to be thankful, ushering in a transformative shift toward a more optimistic thought process and overall perspective.

Gratitude, akin to a transformative thread, intricately weaves beauty into the fabric of our life story. It gently refines our thought processes, guiding them toward optimism and profound appreciation, eventually leaving a good and lasting impression on our outward expressions, which are manifested as the warmest of smiles and acts of kindness.

Make Your Story Beautiful with Respect

Respect is a fundamental aspect of humanity, forming the basis of any healthy relationship, whether it's in a family, among friends, or within a romantic partnership. It involves acknowledging and embracing individual differences and appreciating the unique qualities that each person brings. While the human thought process undergoes continual evolution and change, the capacity to express respect remains a crucial element for maintaining a positive outlook on life. Respectful behavior plays a vital role in establishing a sense of safety and security among individuals, enabling them to forge significant and meaningful relationships with one another.

One of the most important aspects of respect is its ability to make a person display beautiful character, particularly facial expressions. In a state of uncontrolled consciousness, one's facial expressions often reveal their genuine emotions. Practicing respect can contribute to keeping these expressions welcoming. For instance, in an uncontrolled emotional state, inner turmoil like distress or anger may readily manifest on your face. Here, an attitude of respectful behavior can effectively check and halt any further escalation of the situation, promoting a sense of comfort within oneself and in the presence of others.

"The power of respect to make a person display beautiful character goes beyond facial expressions."

Respectful behavior can also help to make a person feel more secure and accepted in any situation. Respectful behavior can play a pivotal role in building bridges between people and can contribute to creating a more harmonious and welcoming atmosphere. Respect is an integral part of the human thought process and essential to building meaningful relationships. Respectful behavior can help ensure that everyone feels safe and secure in any situation, and it can also help make a person display beautiful character, particularly facial expressions.

We must all strive to show respect to one another and ensure that we are creating a positive and accepting atmosphere for everyone. Everyone has a story to tell; make your story beautiful and outstanding with respect.

Here are a few tips.

It can be easy to get caught up in the hustle and bustle of life and forget to be respectful. However, taking the time to show respect to everyone, we can make our lives more meaningful and beautiful. Respectful behavior is the cornerstone of any strong relationship and can be essential in building a positive life story.

First and foremost, respect starts with us. We must learn to treat ourselves with the same respect that we show others. Self-respect is essential in developing a positive attitude and outlook on life. Once we have established a level of respect for ourselves, it will be easier to extend that respect to people we encounter in our daily lives. Respectful behavior also involves showing consideration for others. This means offering our time and attention to those who need it and being mindful of how our actions might affect others. Taking the time to listen to others and consider their feelings is a great way to show respect. We can also demonstrate respect by consistently being honest and open in our communications with others.

Respect is often best shown through actions. We can show respect for others by being kind and compassionate in our interactions. This can come in the form of acts of service, such as offering to help with a task or providing a listening ear. By showing respect to ourselves and those we encounter, we can create meaningful relationships and positive experiences.

"Respectful behavior is the cornerstone of any strong relationship and can be essential in building a positive life story. Start today and make respect a part of your life."

Make Your Story Beautiful with Conversation

We've all heard the saying, "words have power," and this is especially true when it comes to the words we say and the human thought process. Our thoughts and words can control how we feel and how others perceive us. Our words can be used to build up or tear down, and our thoughts can be used to create or destroy. When we are in a state of uncontrolled consciousness, the words we say and the thoughts we think have a huge impact on our character display, especially our facial expressions. Our appearance and the emotions displayed on our faces frequently mirror our inner state of mind.

When our thoughts and words are positive and uplifting, we tend to have pleasant and inviting facial expressions. We often look relaxed and content, which can be very influential in how others perceive us. On the other hand, if our thoughts and words are negative and destructive, our facial expressions will usually reflect this. We tend to look tense and stressed, and this can be very off-putting to the curious onlooker. To have a beautiful character display, it is important that we focus on positive and uplifting thoughts and words. This can help us to maintain a pleasant and inviting facial expression, no matter what the situation. We should also strive to be aware of our thoughts and words and ensure they are not having negative effects on our face.

It is also important to remember that our facial expressions are influenced not only by our thoughts and words but also by other factors. Our environment, relationships, and physical health can all significantly impact our facial expressions. Therefore, it is important to pay attention to these factors and strive to create a positive environment where we can be our best selves. Recognize that the story on our face in these uncontrolled states isn't always perceived as beautiful. Negative or distressing thoughts can manifest as expressions of tension, worry, or sadness, potentially leading to misinterpretation by others.

Conversations can provide an opportunity to bridge the gap between our internal narrative and our external expression. When we engage in open, authentic, and empathetic conversations with others, we have the chance to share the stories behind our uncontrolled expressions. We can provide context, share our thoughts and emotions, and create mutual understanding, transforming our outward expression that might seem less than beautiful into a meaningful and relatable part of our story.

By focusing on positive thoughts and words, and being mindful of our environment and relationships, we can ensure that we are displaying a beautiful character through our facial expressions. This can be a very powerful tool in conveying our inner state of mind and helping others to perceive us in a positive light. We all have a unique story to tell. How it is perceived and how we relate it truly matters. So, endeavor to make your story beautiful through conversation.

Here are a few tips.

Choose what you say, your words have power, and what you say can profoundly affect how your life story is told.

Make a conscious effort to speak positively; it can help to create a beautiful atmosphere in our lives. It's important to avoid negative self-talk and speak kindly to us and to others. Focusing on the positive aspects of a situation and expressing gratitude can help to turn a potentially negative experience into something more positive. Choose our words carefully. We should strive to speak truthfully but with kindness and understanding.

Being mindful of how our words can affect others can help us to be more empathic and compassionate. Remember that our words are powerful tools for creating a beautiful life story. We can choose to use them to spread kindness and joy or to spread negativity and hurt. If we endeavor to make conscious choices about what we say, and how we say it, we can create a life story that is truly beautiful.

The beauty of conversation lies in the way it reflects the thoughts, emotions, and ideas that traverse our minds. When we engage in meaningful and authentic conversations, our thoughts are given a voice, and our outward expressions become the canvas upon which our stories are painted. Conversations become a vital tool for shaping the beauty of our expressions, even in moments of uncontrolled consciousness. They allow us to connect, empathize, and support one another, fostering understanding and compassion. When we share the stories behind our expressions, we invite others into our inner worlds, creating opportunities for deeper connections and greater empathy.

Conversations, then, become the brushstrokes that add depth and color to the canvas of our uncontrolled expressions, making them not only beautiful but also meaningful and enriching for our shared human experience.

Thoughts, when expressed through conversation, can be transformative. They have the potential to inspire, challenge, and connect us with others on profound levels. When we express thoughts of kindness, empathy, and understanding, our outward expressions radiate with warmth and compassion. Our faces light up with genuine smiles, our voices carry the melody of sincerity, and our body language exudes openness.

These expressions not only enhance our stories but also foster meaningful connections with those we interact with. Start today and make your story beautiful with conversation.

Make Your Story Beautiful with Forgiveness

Forgiveness is one of the most powerful tools that humans possess. It can be used to bridge the gap between people who have been hurt or wronged in some way and those who have caused the hurt or wrong. On a deeper level, forgiveness can be seen as a way for us to let go of the past and move forward in our lives.

When we forgive, we acknowledge that we have been hurt or wronged, but we also recognize that this does not define our identity. Instead, we acknowledge the hurt and choose to let it go and move on. This can be incredibly difficult, especially if the hurt or wrong was traumatic or deeply wounding. However, when we choose to forgive, we allow ourselves to be liberated from the past and open to a new possibility of living.

The process of forgiving can also be seen as a journey into the depths of our own consciousness. As we forgive, we can become more aware of our own thoughts and feelings and how they affect our behavior. We can become more aware of our biases and prejudices and how they influence our interactions. We can become more aware of our capacity to love and be compassionate and how our actions affect others. The process of forgiving can also bring about positive changes in our facial expressions. When we forgive, our faces can become more relaxed and peaceful as we no longer carry the burden of resentment or anger. As our empathy grows, we naturally become more receptive to diverse expressions.

Through forgiveness, we can become more tolerant of others and more accepting of our own imperfections. We can learn to be more understanding of the mistakes of others and to show more patience and kindness in our interactions with them. This can enhance our appeal to others, as our authentic care and acceptance, even in the face of their mistakes, are evident in our body language and facial expressions.

Forgiveness is an incredibly powerful tool and one that can bring about immense transformation in our lives. By allowing ourselves to forgive, we can open up to a new level of consciousness and become more aware of our own thoughts and feelings. We can also experience great shifts in our facial expressions as we learn to be more tolerant and accepting of others. Through the act of forgiveness, we can transform ourselves, becoming more beautiful both inside and out. We all have a unique story to share, and forgiveness is the key to making your story truly beautiful.

Here are a few tips.

In the journey of life, we encounter both joyous and challenging moments. While some experiences can be tough, painful, or even heart-wrenching, it is within our power to craft a beautiful narrative by embracing forgiveness.

Forgiveness is a powerful tool that allows us to move on with our lives. It is a way of freeing ourselves from the pain, anger, and hurt associated with the past. It is a way of letting go of negative emotions that can hold us back from living a healthy and fulfilling life. When we forgive, we choose to let go of our resentment and feelings of hurt. We decide to move forward from the painful situation, embarking on the path of healing. We can opt for a more compassionate and understanding perspective, both towards ourselves and those who may have harmed us. Is this a challenging decision?

"When we choose to forgive, we open up the possibility
of building a bridge between the person who hurt us and us."

We are no longer separated by our hurt feelings but instead can start to rebuild the relationship. We can create a new and healthier relationship that is based on understanding, compassion, and trust. Forgiveness can also help us to be kinder to ourselves. It can help us be more compassionate and understanding towards ourselves and our struggles. We can start to practice self-love and self-care and make decisions that will yield a positive outward expression and will help us live our life to its fullest potential.

When we make a conscious choice to forgive, we can make our life story beautiful. We can write a story of hope, growth, and resilience that will inspire others and will serve as a reminder of how powerful we can be when we choose to forgive. Start today and make your story beautiful with forgiveness.

Make Your Story Beautiful with a Smile

A smile is a remarkable instrument for transforming the story our face tells, particularly when we find ourselves in an uncontrolled state of consciousness, deeply immersed in our thoughts. It is an expression that transcends language barriers, radiating warmth, positivity, and a sense of connection. When we allow a genuine smile to grace our face, it not only reflects the beauty within our thoughts but also has the power to shape and amplify that internal narrative.

In those special moments when we are captivated by our thoughts, our facial expressions often mirror the emotions and intensity of our inner dialogue. A smile, however, can change the complexion of this story, infusing it with a sense of joy and optimism. It signifies that our thoughts are positive, light-hearted, or inspiring, even during moments of deep reflection. A smile can soften the lines of concentration, ease tension, and convey a sense of inner contentment, making our uncontrolled expressions not just beautiful but also inviting and engaging.

Moreover, a smile reflects our choice to embrace positivity and share it with the world. It's an outward expression of our inner well-being and our willingness to connect with others in a positive and uplifting way. When we intentionally choose to smile in uncontrolled states of consciousness, it sends a powerful message to ourselves and those around us: that our thoughts are aligned with joy, that we appreciate the moment, and that we are open to sharing our inner beauty with the world. In this way, a simple smile becomes a beautiful and transformative element in the story our face tells, bridging the gap between our internal narrative and our external expressions.

It is an essential part of the human thought process. It has been shown to be one of the most important facial expressions and one of the most powerful communication tools we have. In fact, it has been suggested that smiling is an integral part of our evolutionary development. When we smile, our brain releases neurotransmitters such as dopamine and serotonin, which are linked to positive emotions. Smiling also triggers the release of endorphins, which can help to reduce stress levels. Not only does smiling have physiological benefits, but it can also have psychological benefits. Smiling can make us feel more confident and secure in our interactions with others. It can help us to make a good first impression, and it can help us to connect with others in a positive way.

Smiling can also be a sign of a beautiful character display. When we smile, we project an image of warmth and openness. People who smile often are seen as more approachable and likable and are more likely to be seen as leaders. It is a great way to show our appreciation for the people in our active environment. It's a way to show our appreciation for the good things in life, and it's a way to show our gratitude for the kindness and support others.

As an essential part of the human thought process, smiling can help us to feel more confident, to make a good first impression, and to show our appreciation for people. Smiling can also be a sign of beautiful character display; it can help us connect with others positively and lift our spirits, create a positive atmosphere, and make us feel better. We all have a story to tell; make the positive choice, make your story beautiful with a smile.

Here are a few tips.

A smile is a simple expression of joy, but it can have far-reaching effects on our physical, emotional, and mental health. When we smile, our body releases endorphins, which are hormones that have a calming and uplifting effect. This can play a role in helping to reduce stress and anxiety, contributing to an improved mood, and even boosting our immune system.

A smile can also help us to create better relationships with others. It conveys friendliness, warmth, and openness, which can make it easier to connect with others. It can also help create a sense of trust and security, leading to more meaningful connections. Smiling can help us focus on the positive aspects of our lives and be more mindful and appreciative of our things. It can empower us to be more confident in our decisions and in our lives. With this perspective, you can create a beautiful narrative of your life, one brimming with joy, love, and laughter.

"Start today and make your story beautiful with a smile."

CHAPTER 7

SMILE, A BLESSING IN DISGUISE

Smile a while and give your face a rest is a phrase I learned in my early days. We used to say it quite frequently and even sing it during occasional school devotional exercises and so on. I grew up hearing it constantly. Initially, it was merely a phrase, something we tended to accept at face value. Little did we realize that a smile could, in fact, turn out to be precisely that, albeit conveying the opposite meaning?

"You can take a smile at face value; without a doubt it will add value to your face."
~~ Inspired ~~.

L. A. Chambers

In everyday scenarios, we commonly perceive face value as accepting something for its inherent truth or genuineness, free from scrutiny or skepticism. For many, a smile is just that – a smile, accepted at face value without deeper contemplation. However, some individuals are attuned to their facial expressions when they smile, yet they might not be fully cognizant of the profound impact that a smile can have, the narrative it conveys, and how the simple act of smiling can truly make our personal story beautiful.

Since I set out on a journey to spot the default face. I realized the magic that happens when a person smiles. It is, quite literally, the game changer in determining how you appear when you are not intentionally observing yourself.

"A smile transforms the contours that sculpt the default face and gives the face a more cheerful demeanor."

The more effort I put into observing this concept of your thoughts shaping your face, the more I realized that no other facial expression could substitute the smile posture. It just works; the face goes to rest consistently, reflects the person's mood, and transmits a certain vibe and energy.

As much as it takes more muscles to frown than to smile, it's not a cause for concern; the little, tiny bit of muscles that are activated when you smile totally transform your default face and aligns your thoughts and emotional response.

"A smile changes the contours in your face, plus, the contours that are formed by a smile are the most pleasant."

It puts your face into "relaxed and cheerful mode," a person looks way better when their face takes a break from the effects of stress and inner turmoil that impact the thought process and emotional response.

The phrase "smile a while and give your face a rest" takes on a whole new meaning to me.

Not only does it make sense now, but it is true it takes more muscles to frond than to smile - a smile creates your most pleasant facial contours -your most pleasant face is what you probably should try to display by default.

A smile can be considered a posed facial expression, meaning it's an expression that is done when you are in a conscious state of mind, as opposed to emotional facial expressions, which are types of expressions that are fed by innate emotional reactions to stimuli and do not pass through the cerebral cortex, leaving no time for consciousness or awareness. This can also lead to Micro expressions, which are considered leakage of our true internal emotions before we have time to become aware of the emotion and possibly control it in one way or another.

During moments of uncontrolled consciousness, like daydreaming, doodling, or zoning out, when we are wholly engrossed in our thoughts, our facial expressions genuinely mirror our innermost selves at that precise moment, without a conscious filter or awareness. In such instances, our faces eloquently narrate a story for the curious onlookers, revealing the depth of our thoughts and emotions.

That facial expression and the way our face looks are presented on an open platter for all to see except the victim, "the owner of the face," and believe me, I can't stress this enough, this facial expression can show up without your permission, in a time and place, telling your story in a way that you would rather not.

"A cheerful face reflects the thoughts and emotional by-products of a glad heart and cultivate a radiant smile."
~~ Inspired ~~.

L. A. Chambers

"It's true in many ways, a smile can light up a room,
and it can be a sign of joy and contentment."

When someone is feeling happy and content, it often shows in their facial expression. Therefore, a smile can be so contagious; it can spread joy to those around it. When it comes to our outward appearance, the one thing that stands out the most is our facial expressions. A cheerful face conveys a message of inner joy and contentment that is difficult to ignore. In today's world, we are often surrounded by various social influence, negativity, and stress, so having a cheerful face can be a source of much-needed positivity or "face lift."

Source of a Cheerful Face

A cheerful face often reflects a radiant smile; it conveys a positive attitude and is a sign of good mental well-being. At some point in life, you may have experienced the good vibes that come with seeing a cheerful face and the delighted default face when a person starts daydreaming, driven by thoughts of creativity, success, and love. But where does this cheer come from? What's the source of this cheerful face? The answer lies in the power of positive thinking and the emotional by-products of a glad heart. It's the product of a heart full of joy and a mind that's at peace.

When we focus on positive thoughts, we create an inner joy that radiates outwardly, giving us a cheerful facial expression. Positive thoughts have the power to transform our mindset and our life, creating a sense of contentment and fulfillment that can be seen in our smiles. When we focus on things that make us happy, it helps us to create a positive outlook that boosts our mood and our attitude. It is this attitude that helps to create a cheerful face.

It is important to maintain a positive mental attitude and filter unhealthy events in life that are input to our thoughts. When we center our attention on gratitude and wholeheartedly being thankful for what we have, it not only aids us in appreciating all the good in our lives but also fosters a profound sense of joy.

When we focus on our words and speak in an uplifting and positive manner, it helps us to create an atmosphere of cheerfulness and positivity. When we take good care of our bodies by eating healthy, exercising, and getting enough rest, our face reflects these with a brighter and more cheerful expression. Having a cheerful face is one of the best gifts we can give to ourselves and to everyone we come in contact with. It displays true joy and tells our story in a manner that will be pleasing to the eyes of the onlooker.

Another important source of a cheerful face is positive self-talk. It is important to talk to yourself in a positive and encouraging way rather than a negative and critical one. Let's start today by focusing on the good in life, never holding a grudge, practicing forgiveness, showing love even when it is difficult, and releasing yourself from emotional stress. Let good cheer surface without restriction and concealment.

A person can achieve a cheerful face only if his or her inner self is contented and happy. A cheerful face is the result of a life full of contentment and joy, a person's attitude and perspective towards life, a person who has a positive outlook on life and who can make the best out of any situation. Such a person will be able to handle situations with a smile and a lighthearted attitude. A healthy lifestyle can be considered as one of those by-products of a glad heart. It is important to maintain a balanced diet, exercise regularly, and get enough rest. An individual who enjoys both physical and mental well-being is inherently more inclined to experience a pervasive sense of cheer in their life.

Surrounding oneself with people who are positive and who bring out the best in one another. when individuals find themselves encircled by supportive and encouraging companions, it has a remarkable propensity to bring out the very best in them and significantly contributes to their ability to maintain a cheerful and radiant countenance. A cheerful face is the result of many different factors, but it all begins with a glad heart and a positive attitude. If a person focuses on living a happy and contented life, he or she will be able to maintain a cheerful face.

Good thoughts, born from a pure heart, act as the wellspring of a cheerful face. These thoughts are like sunbeams that dispel clouds of negativity and cast a warm and inviting glow. When we think positively, our faces naturally reflect this inner harmony. Our smiles evolve from being not merely a polite social gesture but to becoming a sincere and spontaneous expression of the genuine happiness we feel within ourselves.

A pure heart, untainted by malice or negativity, forms the foundation for a genuine and radiant smile. When our hearts are free from bitterness, grudges, and ill-will, it allows us to cultivate a mindset filled with optimism, kindness, and love. In this way, the source of a cheerful face is an intricate interplay of our innermost thoughts and the purity of our hearts. It serves as a reminder of the connection between our internal landscape and our external expressions, demonstrating that genuine positivity and joy radiate from the heart, illuminating our faces and inviting others to share in the beauty of our optimism.

Cultivate a Glad Heart

"Every output has a source.
What's the source of your outward expression?"
~~ Inspired ~~.

L. A. Chambers

We all know that a radiant smile can brighten up a room and make us feel better, but do you know that cultivating a glad heart is one of the key sources of a radiant smile?

A glad heart is a state of mind that is focused on the joy and peace that comes from living in the present moment and being grateful for the life we have. It's a mindset that allows us to be content and happy, even in difficult situations.

On the other hand, when your heart feels heavy and burdened, it can show on your face. People can often tell when something is wrong, even if you're trying to hide it. Therefore, it's so important to take care of your heart and make sure it's filled with love and joy. So how do we cultivate a glad heart?

It's like building a tower of memories and a skyscraper of habits that can withstand the seismic events of life and bring you cheer. It's practice, it takes time but will be worth it in the end.

A glad heart is one that is filled with joy and contentment. It is a state of mind that is free from worry, fear, and anger. When we cultivate a glad heart, we become more open to experiencing the beauty of life and the joy of living. This openness allows us to be more present at the moment, savoring all that life has to offer. It will also help us to be more grateful and appreciative of the good that is around us. We cease taking things for granted and instead make a conscious shift in our focus, directing our attention towards the numerous positives and blessings we have in our lives. This transformation in perspective is instrumental in helping us to be more compassionate and understanding individuals.

Having a glad heart also helps us to be more confident and secure in ourselves. We become less affected by the judgments and opinions of others, and instead, we focus on our own self-worth. We become more comfortable in our own skin and learn to accept ourselves for who we are. This newfound confidence and security radiate from within, which leads to a type of facial expression that brings much delight. The facial contours that are sculpted from a truly glad heart are an expression of pure joy, love, and contentment. It is a face that transmits good vibes and smiles that are infectious and ones that can light up any room. So, if you want to be the source of a cheerful and radiant smile, if you want to transform your default face, start by cultivating a glad heart. Spend time each day reflecting on all that you are grateful for and the beauty of life. Spend time appreciating the small moments and savoring the joy of living. Do what make you feel content and secure in yourself.

Cultivating a glad heart is a practice that can be incredibly rewarding and can be done through various means, such as gratitude, mindfulness, and reflection. Practicing gratitude is a powerful way to cultivate a glad heart; it helps us to recognize the positive aspects of our life, no matter how small they may be. We can take time each day to think of the things we are grateful for, and we can also express our gratitude to others.

Mindfulness is another useful practice for cultivating a glad heart. When we are mindful, we can experience all of our emotions, no matter how uncomfortable they may be. We can acknowledge our feelings without judgment and accept them as they are. This can help us to stay in touch with our true selves and cultivate a deeper sense of inner peace. Reflection is also an important practice for cultivating a glad heart. Taking time to reflect on the events of the day can help us to gain perspective, recognize our progress, and celebrate our successes. It can also help us to identify any areas of our life that may need improvement and make changes accordingly. Cultivating a glad heart is a powerful practice that not only brings us joy but enables us to experience the beauty of a genuine smile.

Cheers to more cheer in your life!

Here are a few more tips:

Practice gratitude every day and take the time to be thankful for the things in your life. Whether it's a beautiful sunrise, a warm hug from a loved one, or a delicious meal, taking the time to be thankful will help put you in a better frame of mind.

Do something that brings you joy. Whether it's playing an instrument, painting, gardening, or going for a walk-in nature, find something that brings you happiness and do it regularly. Spend time with positive people. Surround yourself with people who support and uplift you. This will help create positive energy and make it easier to maintain a glad heart.

Speak kindly to yourself. Negative self-talk can be damaging to your mental health and make it difficult to cultivate a glad heart. Instead, practice positive self-talk and give yourself encouragement and love. Take care of your body. A healthy body leads to a healthy mind, so make sure to eat nutritious foods, get enough sleep, and exercise regularly. Cultivating a glad heart is one of the cornerstones and catalyst of producing positive and healthy thoughts, that in turn, give rise to beautiful expressions on the face even when we are not looking.

When we consciously nurture a sense of gladness within ourselves, we create a fertile ground for positive thoughts to flourish. These healthy thoughts guide our perception of the world, helping us see beauty in even the simplest opportunity. Consequently, our faces naturally reflect this inner positivity, radiating with genuine smiles and expressions of contentment.

Building Facial Stamina

Your face is one of the first things people will notice about you. This makes the importance of having a good facial expression that conveys a sense of confidence and openness and tells a story of joy and inner peace all the more important. One way to achieve this is to build up your facial stamina by making smiling a regular habit.

Smiling is a powerful tool. It's been shown to increase your attractiveness to others, reduce stress, and even boost your immune system. So why not make it a regular part of your day?

When it comes to developing facial stamina, the most important thing is to make smiling a habit. This doesn't mean forcing a smile or plastering one on your face all the time, but rather becoming more conscious of when and why you are smiling. When you're out in public, try smiling at people you pass by or even just smiling at yourself in the mirror. Smiling is contagious and can easily spread to others, making it a great way to brighten someone's day. When you're at home or in a private setting, it's important to practice smiling too. Simply allocate a few minutes each day to deliberately focus on your face and intentionally smile. As you consistently practice this, you will gradually begin to notice that your face feels notably more relaxed and your smile becomes increasingly genuine, reflecting a true inner state of contentment.

It is important to be aware of your facial expressions. When you're in a situation where you feel uncomfortable or anxious, instead of frowning or scowling, try to maintain a neutral expression or even a small smile. This will help to build up your facial muscles and make it easier to smile in more difficult situations. Think about facial stamina as the ability to maintain a facial expression, such as a smile, for an extended period without becoming uncomfortable or fatigued. What if we could develop this ability and add it to the skill section of our professional profile? I believe it would be a skill that could be useful in many professional careers and organizations where the face of the business depends on people interaction. I think the ability to maintain a cheerful face that exhibits a radiant smile for an extended period of time would be an important skill set to have, especially, for example, professional actors and models, as well as those in customer service and sales, who often have to maintain a pleasant expression while interacting with customers. But nevertheless, it matters for everyone to practice their facial muscles to display their most pleasant appearance, as this might be your true blessing in disguise.

If your face, by default, is trained to display your most pleasant demeanor, most likely it will, even when you are not thinking about yourself; if you ask me, I will say it does matter! We know the importance of having a strong and healthy body, but have you ever thought about building facial stamina by making smiling a habit? It might sound a bit strange, but I believe it's a great concept and a beneficial way to improve your countenance and overall health, both mentally and physically.

Smiling is one of the most powerful ways to make a positive impression on someone, whether it be a friend, family member, or even a stranger. Unfortunately, many of us don't smile as much as we should or as much as we can. If we make it a habit, however, it can help make us appear more confident and approachable, boosting those cheerful facial muscles to become stronger and your smile to become more genuine.

To start with, you'll want to begin by smiling at yourself in the mirror each morning and evening. This has the bonus of helping you foster a more positive attitude and outlook on life.

You can also try smiling during mundane tasks, like washing dishes or taking out the garbage. This will help you develop a habit of smiling in general, which will become easier to do when it is required in more social or professional settings. Practice smiling with others. You can initiate a conversation with a stranger or a cashier and try to make eye contact and smile. This will help you build up your facial muscles and become accustomed to expressing yourself in a friendlier way.

Overall, building up your facial stamina by making smiling a regular habit can have tremendous benefits and can even make your day-to-day life more enjoyable. So why not give it a try? Fortunately, it's possible to build facial stamina by practicing smiling. Here are some more tips to get you started:

Making smiling a habit can be a great way to build facial stamina and improve your overall health. Start by making a conscious effort to smile throughout the day. Set reminders on your phone or in your calendar to remind you to smile. You can also practice smiling in the mirror each morning as you get ready for your day. Start small. Begin by simply smiling for a few seconds at a time. Once you're comfortable with that, gradually increase the amount of time you're able to sustain the smile.

Focus on the muscles. When you smile, focus on the muscles that are involved in the expression. Make sure you're engaging the muscles around your eyes, lips, and cheeks. This will help you maintain the smile for longer.

Be mindful. As you practice, pay close attention to how your facial muscles are feeling. This will help you identify any areas that are beginning to tire and give you an idea of how long you can maintain the smile. Take breaks. When your facial muscles start to tire, take a break. Take a few deep breaths, relax your face, and then resume your practice. It's important to take care of your face. Make sure to keep your skin clean and moisturized, as this can help to keep your facial muscles toned and improve your overall appearance.

By following these tips and regularly practicing smiling, you can build up the facial stamina necessary to maintain a pleasant expression for an extended period. This skill can be invaluable in professional settings, so make sure to take the time to practice and build your facial stamina. Get your smile game on! It is one of the easiest and most natural ways to instantly boost your mood. A simple smile cannot only put you in a better frame of mind, but it can also have a positive effect on the people around you. It has been shown that smiling can reduce stress, lower blood pressure, and boost your immune system. In addition to the physical benefits, smiling can also have a positive impact on your thought process, and improve your cognitive performance. It has been linked to an increase in creativity, focus, and problem-solving. This, my friend, will help to improve your overall outlook on life. Start today, give yourself a boost, try to make smiling a habit.

Building facial stamina involves the practice and training of our facial muscles to maintain a smile over extended periods. Much like physical endurance, this concept applies to our facial expressions, particularly smiling. By consciously and deliberately training ourselves to smile, we can enhance our ability to convey warmth and positivity even in challenging situations. This practice makes our smiles more genuine and allows us to navigate social interactions with greater ease and grace. Over time, building facial stamina transforms our smiles into a natural and authentic part of our outward expression, making our interactions with others more uplifting, fostering a positive atmosphere.

CHAPTER 8

THE CONCEPT OF PRIORITIZED THINKING

The Things That *"Are"*

The idea of thinking about the things that *"are"* can be a powerful tool when it comes to uncovering your true self and unlocking a beautiful facial expression. Consider the things that *"are"* as the things that we strategically choose to think about, the things that we prioritize and bring to the forefront of our thought process that is vital and important for life, love, success, happiness, and peace of mind. In a world brimming with distractions and societal expectations, it can often be challenging to maintain our focus on the things that hold the utmost importance in our lives. Nevertheless, by consciously taking a moment to pause, reflect, and thoughtfully contemplate the existing circumstances and realities, you can effectively tap into a deeper level of self-awareness and profound understanding.

The beauty of life lies in the present moment, a place where we can be truly authentic and open to the possibilities of our lives. But too often, we get caught up in the past or the future and forget to appreciate the present. Thinking about the things that can help us reconnect with our true selves and access a deeper level of understanding and appreciation.

"Think first on the things that "are." These are the things that are vital and important for life, love, success, happiness, and peace of mind."
~~ Inspired ~~.

L. A. Chambers

When most people think about their true inner selves and the things that are, they assume it's all about the outside. We think about our physical appearance, how we dress, and how we look at others. But what if there was more to it? What if there was a deeper connection between our true inner self and the things that are? The truth is our true inner self is much more than just our physical appearance. It's our thoughts, feelings, and beliefs. It's our values and our purpose. It's the energy that drives us to do the things we need to do in order to live a meaningful and fulfilled life. It helps to form our intellectual Intelligence.

When we take the time to connect with our true inner self and the things that are, we can start to really understand ourselves. We can become more aware of our thoughts, feelings, and beliefs. We can start to understand our purpose and our values.

"We can start to recognize the things that bring us joy and the things that make us feel fulfilled."

As we become more connected with our true inner self and the things that are, we can start to see the beauty in our life. We can start to experience more joy and contentment. We can start to look at ourselves and the people we encounter in a different light. Our outlook on life can start to change, and our facial expressions can become one of contentment and peace.

When we think about the things that are, we can start to recognize the beauty that exists within us. This renewed awareness can lead to a beautiful facial expression that reflects the inner peace and joy that has been found. The expression on our faces can become a reflection of the love, joy, and peace that already exists within us. So, if you're looking for a way to bring more beauty into your life, start by taking the time to connect with your true inner self and the things that are. Spend time getting to know yourself and your values. Connect with the things that bring you joy and the things that make you feel fulfilled.

Allow yourself to experience the beauty that can come from connecting with your true inner self and the things that are. And watch as your facial expression starts to take on a whole new level of beauty and cheer. This achievement will give affirmation to the euphemism "beauty is in the eyes of the beholder."

The Things That Are True

As humans, we all strive to uncover the truth in our lives. We want to know what is real, what is true, and what really matters. We search for answers, questioning and exploring our innermost desires and thoughts to gain a better understanding of ourselves and our place in the world. Often, however, what we think to be true often turns out to be nothing more than a deception. At times, we can be misled by the labyrinth of our own thoughts or by external influences that surround us.

To gain an understanding of ourselves and to realize our innermost true selves, we must put forth the effort to search deep inside ourselves and to think about the things that are true. By thinking about the things that are true, we can gain a much clearer understanding of ourselves and our purpose in life. We can then look at our life in a more positive light and begin to manifest our true potential. We can also begin to understand our own emotions and start to recognize the beauty that lies within each of us.

"When we think about the things that are true and recognize our own inner beauty, it can help to create a beautiful facial expression." We can become more confident in ourselves and our abilities and recognize the worth that lies within us. We can also start to recognize the beauty in others with more compassion and understanding. Thinking about the things that are true can be a powerful tool for finding our true selves.

By recognizing our inner beauty and truth, we can begin to tap into our potential and lead a more fulfilling life. So, take a moment, think about the things that are true, and discover the beauty and the power that lies within. The power of true thought, however, is often overlooked and under-appreciated. We often focus on what is happening outside of us, but there is great power in focusing on the things that are true.

"Thinking about these truths can bring us closer to our true inner selves and cultivate a beautiful, genuine smile."

When we focus on the things that are true, we can step back and understand our lives and our circumstances in a more objective way. We can recognize our blessings, our talents, and our strengths. We can acknowledge our struggles and our weaknesses but can also understand that we are stronger and more capable than we give ourselves credit for. Focusing on truth can help us to appreciate and recognize our true value. When we do this, we can start to see the beauty in our lives, we can recognize and appreciate the small moments and the big ones as well.

We can start to feel more connected to ourselves. This connection leads to a more positive outlook and can help to cultivate a beautiful facial expression. When we focus on the things that are true, we can start to become more self-aware. We can learn to be more mindful and present in our lives. We can explore our emotions and feelings and gain a better understanding of ourselves. This can help us to feel more confident and secure in who we are, leading to inner peace and contentment. This inner peace reflects in our facial expressions to cultivate a genuine smile. When we are connected to ourselves and others, we can smile from the inside out. Our smiles can reflect our inner peace and our appreciation for life, and the many blessings we enjoy.

"Thinking about the things that are true can bring us closer to our true inner selves and cultivate a beautiful, genuine smile."

It can help us to be more self-aware and to appreciate our lives. When we focus on truth, we can gain a better understanding and appreciation of who we are and be more confident in our own skin. This self-confidence and inner peace can be reflected in our facial expressions, leading to a beautiful, genuine smile.

Thinking about the things that are true, focusing on facts and reality rather than dwelling on negativity or distorted perceptions, is a fundamental step in producing healthy thoughts and habits that lead to a beautiful expression on our face. Truth-based thinking promotes clarity, objectivity, and a positive state of mind. When our thoughts are grounded in truth, we tend to nurture a more balanced and optimistic perspective on life. This, in turn, influences our habits, fostering a habit of mindful positivity and gratitude, often adorned with genuine smiles and expressions of contentment that reflect the beauty of our truth-based outlook on life.

The Things That Are Lovely

It is no secret that a beautiful face is one that radiates happiness, confidence, and contentment. But how do we get to this point of inner joy and peace? The answer is simple: by thinking about and focusing as much as we can on the things that are lovely. Thinking about the things that are lovely is a way to cultivate a more positive attitude and outlook on life. It helps us to focus on the good instead of the bad, to appreciate and be grateful for what we have. It is a way to put aside the worries and stresses of life and instead divert our attention on the things that matter, the things that have a positive impact on our lives.

When we think about the things that are lovely, we are allowing ourselves to connect with our true inner selves. We are allowing ourselves to embrace the beauty of life and to be open to the possibilities that it offers. This inner connection can lead to a more beautiful facial expression, one that is full of joy, contentment, and confidence. Focusing on the lovely things in life, we are more likely to have a positive attitude and outlook. We are more likely to be kind to people and to see the beauty in the world.

> "This can lead to a more beautiful facial expression,
> one that is full of life and love."

Thinking about the things that are lovely can be a powerful way to cultivate a more positive attitude and outlook on life. It can help us to connect with our true inner selves and to be open to the possibilities that life offers. This inner connection can lead to a more beautiful facial expression full of joy, contentment, and confidence. So, take the time to think about the things that are lovely, and let your true inner beauty shine through. It's no surprise that when we think about things that are lovely, our facial expressions can change quickly. We can go from a frown or a blank stare to a bright and beautiful smile in an instant. This is because thinking about the things that are lovely is deeply connected to our true inner selves.

When we think about the things that are lovely, we tap into a part of ourselves that is often overlooked in daily life. This part of us is filled with joy, gratitude, and peace.

We can access these feelings and express them through our facial expressions. This can result in a beautiful and gentle smile that is contagious and can even brighten up a room. We can cultivate this beautiful facial expression by consistently thinking on the things that are lovely. We can do this by reflecting on moments of joy or gratitude that we've experienced or by appreciating the beauty of nature or other people.

In addition to thinking about the things that are lovely, we can also practice smiling exercises. This can help us to develop and maintain beautiful facial expressions. We can start by smiling at ourselves in the mirror, then smiling at a loved one, and finally smiling at a stranger. Practicing this can help us not only to open our hearts but also to radiate joy to everyone we encounter. Focusing on the things that are lovely aids in nurturing a beautiful facial expression and carries a remarkable influence on our lives. It's a pathway to feeling more deeply connected, and as we bask in the benefits of contemplating the lovely aspects of life, we can relish the experience of expressing our genuine selves through a warm and beautiful smile.

Contemplating the things that are lovely constitutes a powerful and transformative practice that can deeply influence our thought patterns, daily habits, and the radiance of our outward expressions. When we consciously and purposefully direct our attention to the beauty, kindness, and positivity that exists in our lives, our thoughts organically gravitate toward these lovely facets. This gradual shift in thinking initiates a ripple effect, fostering a mindset inherently characterized by boundless optimism, profound gratitude, and a heightened appreciation for life's abundant simple pleasures.

As we consistently devote our thoughts to the contemplation of the things that are lovely, these positive thoughts actively mold our daily habits. We naturally find ourselves more inclined to partake in acts of kindness, actively seek out opportunities for beauty, and intentionally create moments that inspire joy and love. These habits, firmly ingrained in our daily routines, continuously reinforce the ongoing cycle of positivity. Consequently, our faces gradually transform into radiant reflections of this inner metamorphosis, adorned with authentic smiles and expressions of warmth, delight, and contentment. Ultimately, the practice of thinking about the things that are lovely not only renders our own lives more beautiful but also leaves a lasting and inspiring impression on the world through the genuine beauty of our outward expressions.

Things That Are Just

Thinking about the things that are just is a practice that aligns our thoughts and habits with principles of fairness, equity, and integrity. When we consciously focus on what is just and right in the world, it cultivates a sense of moral clarity and responsibility within us. This thought process encourages us to make choices and develop habits that promote justice and fairness in our own actions, interactions, our general approach to life and dealing with people.

Let's talk: it's a conversation that speaks to the power of our own inner thoughts and how they shape the cosmos. Thinking on the things that are just is an important part of self-reflection and self-awareness. It helps us to stay grounded in our true selves. When we think on the things that are just, we are actively engaging in the act of self-reflection. This helps us to recognize our own strengths and weaknesses and to better understand our motivations and desires. Thinking about the things that just give us insight into our own values and beliefs helps us to make decisions that align with our core values. This type of self-reflection can help us to recognize our own biases and preconceived notions and helps us strive for open-mindedness.

As we consistently think about the things that are just, we become more inclined to stand up for what is right, advocate for the marginalized, and contribute to a more equitable society. These habits not only shape our character but also influence the beauty of our outward expressions. When we champion justice and fairness, our faces often reflect a sense of moral strength, determination, and even a serene beauty born from the knowledge that we are aligned with principles that promote a better world. In this way, thinking about the things that are "just" not only contributes to our own inner well-being but also enhances the beauty of our expressions as a reflection of our commitment to a just and equitable world.

Thinking about the things that are just can also lead to a beautiful facial expression. When we think about things that are just, we are actively engaging in the act of self-love. Engaging in this practice aids us in recognizing our own intrinsic worth and empowers us to appreciate the distinctive qualities that make us unique. When we consciously think about things that embody justice and fairness, we naturally become more predisposed to approach life with an open and overwhelmingly positive attitude.

"This helps us to maintain a sense of optimism and joy,
which can be reflected in our outward
expressions and behavior."

Thinking about the things that are just is an important part of self-reflection and self-awareness. It helps us to stay grounded in our true selves, and it can lead to beautiful facial expressions. When we think about the things that are just, we are actively engaging in the act of self-love, and this can help us to recognize our own worth and to appreciate our own unique qualities. Thinking about the things that just allow us to make decisions that align with our core values and to approach life with an open and positive attitude. All these factors can help us to maintain a sense of personal fulfillment.

We all have a true inner self, a part of us that is our authentic self and remains unchanged regardless of the situation. When we tap into our true inner selves, we often find peace, love, and joy that can be expressed through our facial expressions. A smile is one of the best expressions of our true inner self, and it's been said that it's one of the most beautiful things in life.

Thinking about the things that are just is one way to access our true inner self and cultivate a smile. Just thinking is a form of meditation, and it can help us to focus on the present moment and the things that are important to us. It is a way to slow down and become aware of our thoughts and feelings and to notice what is real and true for us. It allows us to access our inner wisdom and recognize our inner power and strength.

When we think about things that are just, we are reminded of our inner truth. We can connect with our highest self and find that place of peace, joy, and love that lies within us. This connection can be expressed through a beautiful facial expression, such as a smile. A warm and genuine smile can serve as an exceptionally powerful tool to effectively communicate our inner truth and our willingness to connect with others. It serves as a means to express the profound joy and love that resides within us.

Thinking about the things that are just is a wonderful way to access our true inner self and cultivate a beautiful facial expression that can lead to a smile. It is a way to honor our inner truth and find peace and joy. It is a way to connect with our highest self and express our inner joy and love to the world.

Aligning our thoughts and habits with principles of fairness, equity, and integrity is an ethical and moral compass that guides our actions and decisions in both our personal lives and interactions with others. It involves a deep commitment to treating all individuals with impartiality and respect, valuing their rights and dignity. Fairness compels us to ensure that everyone is given an equal opportunity, without discrimination or bias. Equity urges us to acknowledge and address disparities, striving for a more level playing field. Integrity calls us to act honestly, transparently, and ethically in all situations, even when no one is watching.

This alignment with these principles reflects a conscious effort to embody values that foster harmonious relationships and a just society. It involves not only recognizing injustices and biases but also taking proactive steps to address them. It may mean advocating for change, supporting social causes, or challenging our own biases and prejudices. In essence, aligning our thoughts and habits with fairness, equity, and integrity means being a force for positive change and promoting a world where the inherent worth of every individual is acknowledged and respected.

It's a journey towards becoming better, both as individuals and as a collective, and this commitment often shines through as a beautiful expression on our faces, a reflection of our dedication to a just and equitable lifestyle for ourselves, positively impacting our endeavors in our home, our community, and the world.

Things That Are Pure

It's said that beauty comes from within, but what does that really mean? It means that our thoughts and attitudes can have a direct impact on how we look physically. Thinking about the things that are pure and how this relates to one's inner true self can lead to a beautiful facial expression that can radiate outwards and affect others in a positive way.

Thinking about the things that are pure is a practice that taps into the essence of innocence, goodness, and simplicity. When we consciously focus on purity in our thoughts, we tend to gravitate toward unadulterated positivity and clarity. This thought process encourages us to let go of the clutter of negativity, cynicism, and complexity that often clouds our minds. Rather than being preoccupied with complexities, we become acutely attuned to the simplicity and the inherent beauty that can be found in life's purest and most unadulterated moments.

Your thoughts and beliefs can be powerful tools when it comes to how we present ourselves to the world. When we focus on positive, pure things, it can lead to a brighter, more energetic, and naturally beautiful expression on our faces. Thoughts of love, joy, and compassion can help us to relax, and our facial muscles will naturally contract in a way that is more pleasing and attractive to the eye. We can also use this same power of thought to help us to look more vibrant and healthier.

It is said that the eyes are the windows to the soul, and that is often true! When we think about the things that are pure, our eyes will sparkle, and our skin will radiate with a beautiful glow. Our eyes will be brighter, more alert, and more inviting. Our skin will be softer and smoother, and our complexion will appear fresher and more youthful.

The power of our thoughts can also have a direct effect on how we feel. When we focus on the things that are pure, we can start to feel lighter, freer, and more alive. Our moods can become more positive and our outlook on life can become brighter. This inner peace and joy will reflect on our faces, and our expressions will become more animated and inviting. This can be an incredibly powerful tool for helping us to feel more confident, attractive, and happier with ourselves and our lives. If we focus on the good, our inner beauty will naturally radiate outwards and affect others in an encouraging and positive way. One of the most profound and powerful things that anyone can do is to think about the things that are pure. This is something that is essential to cultivate some cheer in our life.

When we think about the things that are pure, we are engaging in deep, meaningful reflection and thought. We are allowing our minds to wander to the places that bring us peace and joy. We are opening ourselves up to the possibility of discovering new truths and ideas. We are allowing ourselves to grow. By thinking about the things that are pure, we are also engaging in the form of mental and emotional cleansing. We are releasing any negative thoughts, feelings, and beliefs that no longer serve us. We are allowing ourselves to let go of any fear, anger, and worry that is weighing us down. We are allowing ourselves to experience the beauty of life that exists around us at any given time.

And when we think on the things that are pure, we are cultivating a beautiful facial expression. We are allowing our faces to relax, to soften, to become a reflection of our inner truth. We are allowing ourselves to smile, to laugh, to enjoy the moment. We are allowing ourselves to be vulnerable and to be seen in all our beauty, in all of our flaws.

Thinking about things that are pure is an act of self-love and self-care. It is a way to connect with our innermost thoughts and feelings and to find a sense of peace and calm. It is a way to become more in tune with our true selves and to bring more beauty into our lives. So, take some time today to think about the things that are pure. Let your mind wander to the places that bring you joy and peace. Allow yourself to be vulnerable and to be seen in all your beauty. And when you do, you will be sure to cultivate a cheerful smile that will light up the world.

The ability to think about the things that are pure is a key component of finding one's true inner self, and with it comes a beauty that radiates from within. A beautiful facial expression, such as a warm and genuine smile, can be cultivated within oneself when one takes the time to focus on the good in life and the things that bring joy.

When we take the time to think about the things that are pure, we are allowing ourselves to tap into our true inner nature. This can be done by taking the time to reflect on the positive aspects of life, the moments that bring us joy and peace. We are opening ourselves up to the profound possibility of forming a deeper and more meaningful connection with our innermost selves, enabling us to recognize and unlock our true potential.

Taking the time to think about the things that are pure can also lead to a more beautiful facial expression. When we focus on the good in life and the things that bring us joy, our facial expressions can become more relaxed and inviting. A genuine smile is often a result of being in a positive mindset, and when we take the time to think about the things that are pure, we can help cultivate a warm and inviting smile that radiates from within.

To cultivate a beautiful facial expression and a genuine smile, it is important to take the time to think about the things that are pure and to connect with our innermost selves. This can be done through activities such as meditation, journaling, or even just taking a few moments to appreciate the beauty of our existence and the ubiquitous influence we have in the world. Taking the time to nurture our inner nature can lead to a more beautiful and inviting facial expression that radiates joy and peace.

Thinking about things that are pure is a key component of connecting with our true inner selves and cultivating beautiful facial expressions. Taking the time to reflect on the positive aspects of life and to nurture our inner nature, we can open ourselves up to the possibility of forming a deeper connection with our true selves and radiating a smile that comes from within.

As we consistently think about the things that are pure, it influences our daily habits. We become more inclined to seek out and create moments of purity in our lives—acts of kindness, moments of stillness, or connections with nature. These habits reshape our daily routines, infusing them with a sense of serenity, kindness, authenticity, and impact our outward expressions.

"Our faces become canvases that reflect this pure
inner transformation, adorned with serene
smiles of genuine goodness."

For me it is a journey, I recall the words "man you should have seen your face a minute ago." The humbling scenario gave me a purpose to break free. I know I have to crave for the "things that are," the things that will enrich my inner world. Those things will also result in a beautiful expression on my face. It's like applying the formula to achieve the outward reflection of the peace, simplicity, and purity that resides within us.

This outward beauty, born from pure and wholesome thoughts and habits, becomes a source of inspiration and positivity for those around us, encouraging them to seek purity and beauty in their own lives as well.

Things That Are of Good Report

Thinking about the things that are of good report is a practice that centers our thoughts and attention on positivity, kindness, and optimism. It involves actively seeking out and focusing on the uplifting and constructive aspects of life, people, and situations. This thought process cultivates a mental landscape marked by hope, encouragement, and a deep appreciation for the goodness that exists in the world. It is an important step in uncovering our true inner self and cultivating a beautiful facial expression. Taking time to focus on the positive can help reduce stress, promote a sense of well-being, and create a positive impression among others.

"To cultivate a smile, it is important to practice gratitude, look for the good in others, and take time for self-care. This should not be an option, after all, if we do not take care of ourselves, we are missing the mark for sustainability."

It is known that thinking about the things that are good can be beneficial to one's mental health. If one is able to focus on the positives, it could help that person build a more positive outlook on life, filter out those unwanted influences of life events which are ingredients to building a skyscraper of healthy habits.

This also can lead to a more positive attitude and can help to improve physical health. A person focuses on the good things they have accomplished, or the good things in their lives, they are more likely to feel more content with themselves. In turn, this can lead to a more positive attitude. It can also lead to a greater sense of self-confidence and self-worth.

A person who is feeling content and confident in themselves is more likely to smile more and be more open with their facial expressions. This can help create a more positive impression of the individual and can help them to make a good impression on others. All these practices and habits can significantly contribute to a person's ability to create a more positive presence, making a favorable impression on others.

Smiling is a fundamental part of how we interact with the world and one another. A smile can convey a wide range of emotions, from joy to sympathy to contentment, and it can even be used as a powerful form of nonverbal communication. While a smile may seem effortless, it takes some effort to cultivate a genuine facial expression that conveys genuine emotion. Thinking about the things that are of good report is one way to create an inner sense of peace and contentment that can lead to a beautiful facial expression.

Being mindful of the present moment and focusing on the things that bring joy can help bring a sense of calm and a genuine smile to one's face. It's important to take time to savor the small moments of life, whether it's the taste of a delicious meal, the warmth of the sun, or the laughter of loved ones.

When the inner self is in a positive and content state, it is easier to cultivate a genuine smile. A higher level of self-awareness can help to recognize the emotions that are being experienced and the thoughts that are running through the mind. Taking a few moments to pause and observe the thoughts and feelings can help to bring a sense of peace and calm to the inner self. Having a positive outlook on life and focusing on the good can also lead to a beautiful facial expression. A smile can be a powerful tool for expressing emotion, and it can also be used to communicate joy, sympathy, and contentment.

"Taking a few moments to focus on the things that bring joy can be a great way to cultivate a genuine smile."

It can be used to communicate a wide range of emotions. Taking a few moments to focus on the things that are of good report and cultivate a positive inner self can lead to a beautiful facial expression and a genuine smile.

It is important to focus on the positive aspects of our lives. We can start by writing down three things that we are grateful for each day. This can help to shift our focus away from the negative and remind us of the good in our lives.

Additionally, we can make a conscious effort to look for the good in others and compliment them often. Doing so can help us to cultivate a sense of appreciation and generate a more positive outlook. The power of thinking about things that are of good report is often overlooked today.

We often focus our attention on the negative and forget to take a step back and focus on the positive. It is important to take time to think about things that are of good report, as this can help us to find our true inner selves and cultivate a beautiful facial expression. we can become more mindful of our thoughts and feelings. This can allow us to connect with our true inner selves and gain a much better understanding of our values and beliefs.

Through this process, we can gain a clearer sense of who we are and what we want out of life. When we consistently think about the things that are of good report, it naturally guides our habits and actions toward creating more of those positive experiences. We become more inclined to offer words of encouragement, extend acts of kindness, and celebrate the achievements and good deeds of others. These habits, rooted in positivity, not only benefit our well-being but also enrich our interactions with those around us.

The impact of thinking about the things that are of good report extends to our outward expressions, particularly our faces. When our thoughts are infused with positivity, our faces often mirror this inner beauty. Genuine smiles, expressions of appreciation, and a welcoming demeanor become characteristic of our interactions with others. This beautiful and genuine outward expression serves as a profound testament to the transformative power of wholeheartedly focusing on the good and uplifting aspects of life. It not only inspires an enduring sense of joy and connection in our relationships but also makes a substantial contribution to fostering a more positive and harmonious life.

CHAPTER 9

SMILE - THE GAME CHANGER

Smiles have been called many things, but *"the game changer"* is my new nickname for a smile. It can turn a bleak situation into a positive one and can be the difference between success and failure in more ways than one. The mission could be social, formal, or professional. Take this one hint to increase your chance for success, *"shake a hand with those nearby and greet them with a smile."*

Smiles have the power to lighten the mood of a room. They can be contagious, giving everyone around a feeling of comfort and joy. It can make you more approachable and make it easier to start a conversation with someone. When people are greeted with a smile, it can set the tone for the entire interaction.

"Going for that deal? Don't worry; you got this."

You've got a great tool for negotiation. The sincere smile, a potent and disarming gesture, possesses the unique ability to often disarm an opponent and make them more willing to compromise. It effectively communicates that you're open to hearing different perspectives and serves as a powerful tool for encouraging people to open up and engage in constructive discussions about their ideas and viewpoints.

"Feeling a bit nervous? Don't worry, you got this!"

It's that smile! It can be a great way to boost your own confidence. When you feel good about yourself, it's easier to approach new situations with a positive attitude. Smiling can help you stay focused on your goals and can help you stay motivated and encouraged even when times are strenuous.

"If you find yourself in a difficult situation, don't forget to smile. It might just be the game-changer you've been looking for."

I have now become an expert in spotting default faces. I see it all the time. People do not have a clue about their facial expression and the story it tells about them. When you are caught in a state of uncontrolled consciousness and start to stare into space, totally captivated by your thoughts, your face, by default, takes a certain shape, and you are now looking the way you are thinking. But a certain magic happens when a person smiles; it totally transforms the contours of the default face. It is literally the game changer of how your face looks. It possesses the magical ability to transform a frown upside down and transform all the negative emotions into positive ones.

When we are feeling hurt, distressed, or upset, our facial expressions can often reflect these emotions. We may furrow our brows, tighten our lips or even frown. But the simple act of smiling can be a great way to change the way we look and how we feel. Smiling has been scientifically proven to help reduce stress and anxiety, as well as make us feel more positive. It signals to the brain that we are happy and can lead to the release of feel-good hormones like endorphins and dopamine.

By the way, let's not take these two words endorphins and dopamine at face value. I did not really learn about endorphins and dopamine until I started to research this concept of the default face and the effect of a smile. I get to understand that they are chemicals (hormones) your body releases when it feels pain or stress. They're released during pleasurable activities such as exercise, massage, eating, and sex too.

Like seriously? I ask myself; "Can a smile do all of this?"

Well, that's not a bad gig. They will help to improve your sense of well-being. Smiling is a simple yet powerful gesture that can change the way you appear to others. It can lift your spirits, brighten someone else's day, and even alter the way people perceive you. Unfortunately, during emotional distress, hurt, grief, and all the other difficult feelings, the act of smiling can often be the last thing on our to-do lists.

However, research suggests that forcing a smile can have a positive effect on our emotional state. Studies have found that smiling, even if not genuine, can reduce levels of stress and increase happiness. In this way, a smile is a potent game changer to how your face looks – regardless of what you're feeling inside.

You may have heard the phrase 'fake it 'til you make it,' and for many of us, this means forcing a smile when we're feeling down. But does forcing a smile really make us feel better, or is it just a way to mask our true emotions?

The act of forcing a smile can have a profound effect on our emotional state. I believe that even if we don't feel like smiling, the simple act of putting a smile on our face can make us feel happier, and make our bodies relax. But forcing a smile can also be a way of masking our true emotions. When we are feeling hurt or distressed, it can be difficult for us to show our true feelings. So, while forcing a smile can make us feel better and benefit our physical health, it can also be a way to mask our true emotions. It's important to remember that while forcing a smile can be helpful in the short term, it's important to find ways to address our true feelings in the long term. Talking to a trusted friend or therapist can help us process our hurt and distress. What's more, smiling can be a great way to put ourselves in a better frame of mind. It can be a reminder to take a step back and appreciate the good things in life.

A smile is indeed the "game changer" in many aspects of our lives, whether in our social or professional endeavors. It holds a unique power to create a positive and lasting impact on those who we encounter. When we strategically employ a smile, it transforms into a potent tool that can significantly increase our chances for success in various aspects of life.

In our professional interactions, a smile is like a universal key that can unlock doors and build bridges. It communicates approachability, confidence, and a positive attitude. Whether in a job interview, a business meeting, or networking event, a genuine smile can set a positive tone, making others more inclined to engage with us. It conveys a deep sense of warmth and authenticity, frequently leaving a memorable and lasting impression on colleagues, clients, or potential employers.

In social settings, greeting somebody with a smile serves as the first transfer of positive energy in any interaction. It immediately puts others at ease and fosters a sense of connection. A smile can defuse tension, break the ice, and create an atmosphere of openness and friendliness. When we approach social situations with a smile, we not only uplift our own spirits but also contribute to a more harmonious and enjoyable environment for everyone involved.

A smile is simple, but an effective tool that can significantly influence the trajectory of our personal and professional lives. It effectively sets the stage for success by creating positive and deeply meaningful connections, while also vividly conveying our positivity and approachability.

Change Your Game, Change Your Style

The ability to smile is truly a blessing and a gift because smiling is one of the most powerful nonverbal expressions of emotion that humans can express. It is an expression of joy and happiness that transcends cultural boundaries. There are indeed many different types of smiles, each carrying its own unique meaning and nuance, and it can sometimes be challenging to fully understand and distinguish the subtle differences between them.

Do you want to change your game? Do you want to communicate your thoughts and how you feel at the moment? Do you want to make the right impression? Then learn how to change your style, change your smile.

"Change your game, change your style, change your smile."
~~ Inspired ~~.

L. A. Chambers

The truth is the world of smiles is wide and varied, and each type of smile expresses something unique. From the wide-eyed smile of joy to the subtle smirk of amusement, the different types of smiles on our faces can tell a lot about how we feel. And while each smile may look different, they all share one common trait - they make us look great!

Here you go!

I bet you didn't realize that there are more than 16 different types of smiles. Time to build up your facial stamina by practicing them and learning how to read them. So! Cheers to one for your mood and your message; communicate it with a cheerful face.

The Duchenne Smile, also known as the genuine or genuine smile, is often considered to be the most authentic type of smile. This type of smile is characterized by a symmetrical lip curvature with both corners of the mouth pulled up toward the eyes. This smile involves the zygomatic major muscles and the orbicularis oculi muscle and is considered the sincerest, associated with joy, and the most effective way to express genuine emotions.

The Social Smile is probably the type of smile that is most often seen in everyday life. This type of smile is often seen in social situations as a way to greet someone or show politeness. It is usually characterized by a slight upturn of the lips but without any crinkling of the eyes.

The Polite Smile is like the Social Smile but is used to express politeness or agreement. This smile is often seen when someone agrees with another, characterized by a slight upturn of the lips but no crinkling of the eyes. It's typically used when feeling socially obligated to respond positively. This type of smile only involves the zygomatic major muscles and not the orbicularis oculi muscle. It appears as a half-hearted attempt at smiling and can be mistaken for disinterest. This is the smile given when not particularly happy but wanting to maintain politeness. It is a subtle, often closed-mouth smile, which is sometimes accompanied by a slight nod of the head.

The Laughing Smile is often used to express joy or happiness. This type of smile is characterized by a broad upturn of the lips and is usually accompanied by a laugh.

The Closed-lip Smile is often used to express politeness or agreement. This type of smile is characterized by a slight upturn of the lips but doesn't involve any crinkling of the eyes.

The tight-lipped smile is another type of smile that is characterized by lips that are drawn tightly together. This type of smile conveys a sense of politeness or awkwardness. It is commonly observed in situations that require politeness but may not necessarily involve friendliness.

The half-smile is a slight smiling gesture that is characterized by one corner of the mouth being pulled up slightly. This type of smile is often seen when someone is trying to be polite but is not necessarily amused. It's a way to maintain decorum in social situations.

The smirk is a type of smile that is associated with arrogance and smugness. This type of smile is characterized by one corner of the mouth being pulled up slightly, and one eyebrow raised. It is often used to convey a sense of superiority or mockery, although it can also indicate amusement or pleasure.

The fake smile is a type of smile that is often used to hide true emotions or to appear polite. This type of smile is characterized by corners of the mouth being pulled up, but without the crinkling of the eyes. It signals a polite or obligatory response.

The sneer is a form of smiling that is often done to show contempt or disapproval. It involves curling up one's lips and raising one corner of the mouth. It can be used to express anger, sarcasm, or criticism. This type of smile often carries a tone of disapproval or mockery.

The smize is a type of smile that involves looking with the eyes rather than with the mouth. It is often used to show confidence and can be used to make a lasting impression.

The cheeky grin is a type of smile that is often done to show playfulness or mischievousness. It is typically done with a wide grin and involves raising both sides of the mouth.

The shy smile. This is the type of smile you'd give someone when you're feeling a little bit shy or embarrassed. It's a closed-mouth smile that's often accompanied by a slight lowering of the eyes. This type of smile can signify shyness or reservation, and it is commonly seen in situations where an individual may feel uncertain or uncomfortable.

The amused smile. This is the type of smile you'd give someone when you're feeling a bit of amusement or irony. It's a closed-mouth smile often accompanied by a slight smirk at the corners of the mouth, giving the impression of someone who may be hiding their true emotions or intentions.

The sarcastic smile. This is the type of smile you'd give someone when you're being a bit sarcastic or making a joke. It's a closed-mouth smile often accompanied by a slight smirk at the corners of the mouth, giving the impression of someone who may be hiding their true emotions or intentions.

When it comes to smiling, it is important to be aware of the different types and how they can be used to communicate the right message. A genuine Duchenne smile can be used to show genuine emotion or happiness. The polite smile is typically used when feeling socially obligated. The sneer, smirk, smize, and cheeky grin can be used to show different types of emotions, such as anger, superiority, confidence, or playfulness. Knowing when to use each type of smile can help you make the right impression and effectively communicate your emotions. No matter which type of smile you choose, it's sure to make you look great and give you several physiological benefits. So, the next time you're feeling happy, embarrassed, amused, or sarcastic, don't forget to give a good old-fashioned smile!

As we discussed earlier, the good old smile should not just be taken as face value, but indeed, it does add value to your face, a means, it can work wonders. I am a testimony to this fact, some may argue that   technical skills and expertise are essential for success, but the impact of a genuine and confident smile should not be underestimated. It is a universal language that transcends barriers and fosters positive connections.

Let's delve deeper into the art of leveraging your smile to excel in your professional pursuits and unravel how this seemingly simple yet profoundly impactful tool can open doors to a multitude of opportunities.

A genuine smile possesses a remarkable ability to transcend barriers and establish connections on a fundamental human level. When you genuinely smile, it communicates a sense of authenticity and sincerity that resonates with others. It conveys your openness and approachability, making it easier for people to engage with you in both formal and informal professional settings.

Interactions can often feel impersonal and transactional, a genuine smile has the power to break down walls and create a warm and welcoming atmosphere. It serves as an invitation for others to approach you, ask questions, or seek your guidance. By radiating positivity through your smile, you can create an environment where people feel comfortable expressing their thoughts, concerns, and ideas, fostering open and constructive communication. A genuine smile reflects your sincere interest in others and your appreciation of their presence and opinions.

In a professional context, this can significantly enhance your ability to build strong relationships with colleagues, clients, and superiors. People are naturally drawn to those who make them feel seen and appreciated, I believe a genuine smile is a tool in accomplishing just that.

"Think of it this way it's like building another layer in the skyscraper of healthy habits."

By consistently wearing a genuine smile, you can cultivate a reputation for being approachable and trustworthy. Colleagues will be more inclined to seek your input or collaborate on projects, clients will feel more at ease discussing their needs, and superiors will appreciate your positive and engaging demeanor. Trust is a cornerstone of successful professional relationships. A genuine smile can go a long way in establishing and nurturing that trust.

Moreover, a genuine smile from a radiant heart of love has a ripple effect that extends beyond individual interactions. When you radiate positivity through your smile, it can uplift the overall atmosphere and morale in that environment. It can create a more cohesive and supportive team environment, where individuals feel valued and motivated. In a work environment, a positive work culture not only fosters collaboration and productivity but also attracts talented individuals who thrive in such an environment, leading to better opportunities for career growth and success.

"This is truly a game changer. If you want to win, then change your game, change your style, capitalize on the power of a genuine smile. This I would say, "cannot be overstated."

It has the ability to create a warm and welcoming atmosphere, make others feel comfortable and at ease, and signal your openness and genuine interest in others. Harness the power of a genuine smile to build strong relationships, foster teamwork, and establish trust in your professional endeavors.

"Embrace the authenticity of your smile and watch as it becomes a catalyst for positive connections and opportunities in your career and professional endeavors."

Harnessing the power of your smile in emotional endeavors can extend far beyond its aesthetic appeal. It possesses the power to uplift our spirits, strengthen our resilience, positively influence our overall well-being, and empower us to navigate life's challenges with grace and positivity. A smile is contagious, transcending language and cultural barriers. It has the remarkable ability to elicit a mirrored response in others, triggering a cascade of positive emotions. This is similar to laughing. I recall the words my colleague said to me "man you should have seem your face a minute ago", as he tries to re-construct the contours of my default face on his face.

The training room environment was immediately transformed from "sneaky grins" to explosive outbursts of laughter. As much as this could result in emotional devastation on my path, the concept is that a smile, as with laughter, can be contagious and change the environment in a hurry.

When we greet someone with a warm and genuine smile, it creates an immediate connection and communicates our openness and friendliness. This simple act has the potential to uplift the mood of others, inspire joy, and generate a sense of well-being. Let's use our smile to spread positivity and contribute to the emotional well-being of those we encounter.

Think of your smile as a beacon of light, dispelling negativity and replacing it with optimism and happiness. It will act as a gentle reminder that there is goodness in us and that small gestures of kindness can make a significant impact.

The ripple effect of a smile extends far beyond immediate interactions. When we uplift someone's spirits with our smile, we never know how that positivity may resonate with them throughout their day. A simple smile can create a chain reaction, inspiring others to share their smiles and spread positivity to those they encounter. It becomes a collective effort to make the world a brighter and happier place.

How about cultivating gratitude and happiness? This may take time, but think of it as a transformative journey, but our smile can play a pivotal role in this process. When we choose to smile, we actively shift our focus towards the positive aspects of life, redirecting our attention from worries and challenges to the blessings and joys that surround us. fuel your smile testosterone, it will eventually become your "go to face", A face with a smile that will serve as a reminder to appreciate the present moment and find happiness in even the simplest of pleasures.

By consciously choosing to smile and express gratitude, we create a powerful feedback loop. Our smile reinforces the feelings of happiness within us, triggering a cascade of positive emotions. It becomes a physical manifestation of our inner joy, radiating outward and inviting more happiness into our lives.

The act of smiling becomes a self-reinforcing cycle, deepening our experience of gratitude and enhancing our overall sense of happiness. I believe when we smile, we are more likely to acknowledge and appreciate the blessings and positive experiences that come our way, focus on abundance rather than scarcity, and focus on goodness rather than challenges. This shift in perspective allows us to cultivate a deeper sense of gratitude for the simple joys, connections, and opportunities that enrich our lives. This phenomenon becomes a magnet for happiness, fostering a more fulfilling and emotionally satisfying life.

I believe our smile acts as a potent antidote to stress and a catalyst for emotional resilience. Through its activation of neural pathways, a smile promotes relaxation and reduces stress levels, we affirm our ability to overcome obstacles and adapt to challenging circumstances. It becomes a powerful reminder of our ability to navigate emotional turmoil with grace and resilience. Smiling builds emotional fortitude, empowering us to face future challenges with confidence. When we intentionally smile, even for a moment, we create a pause in the intensity of our emotions. This momentary break allows us to gather our thoughts, regulate our breathing, and approach the situation with a clearer and more composed mind. It helps us maintain a sense of balance and prevents stress from overpowering our emotional well-being.

Let's practice a gentle smile during challenging moments, tap into our innate emotional resilience, regain perspective, and navigate difficulties with state of mind that is much calmer. Embracing the power of a smile I believe will enable us to counteract stress, maintain composure, and cultivate emotional well-being even in the face of adversity.

I have been converted, I am on journey to become one of the biggest cheerleaders to encourage others to fuel their "smile testosterone" and watch the effect of a smile as they pursue their endeavors. It's truly a game changer, I guess we can agree that winning in your relationship, intimate and love endeavors involve nurturing meaningful connections, prioritizing communication, and active listening, it could also involve cultivating trust, empathy, and understanding. Investing time, effort, and emotional energy into building a strong foundation and creating shared experiences is by no means discounted.

In a similar manner a smile can be a powerful tool that can help you win in your intimate and love endeavors. It has the ability to convey warmth, attraction, and affection, setting the stage for a deeper emotional connection with your partner. In simple terms "it looks good on you, your face becomes a delight, think about it, what if your "default face" was a beauty in the eyes of the beholder in those times when it matters most, that would be a game changer.

I believe that if a smile is used effectively, you can enhance your romantic interactions, create a positive atmosphere, and build a strong foundation of love and happiness.

A genuine smile can communicate your interest and desire for your partner. It serves as a non-verbal signal of attraction, drawing them closer and making them feel desired, this creates an inviting and comfortable space for open communication, intimacy, and vulnerability. A powerful thing indeed, that can melt away any reservations or insecurities, allowing your partner to feel safe and valued in your presence.

Beyond attraction, a smile can also play a vital role in fostering emotional connection and understanding. When you smile, you demonstrate warmth and affection, expressing your love and care for your partner. A genuine smile can effectively diffuse tension, lighten the mood, and create a positive atmosphere during moments of disagreement or conflict. It conveys a genuine willingness to listen and understand, encouraging open and honest communication.

By using your smile to create a nurturing and supportive environment, you can deepen your emotional bond and strengthen the love you share. Notwithstanding the fact that it is contagious as we mentioned earlier in this book, it has the power to uplift the mood of both you and your partner. It's one of the most beautiful things is a genuine smile from a heart of love, it can create a ripple effect of positivity and happiness. It can turn an ordinary moment into a joyful one, infusing your relationship with lightheartedness and laughter, be a source of comfort and reassurance, and remind your partner that they are loved and cherished.

It helps create lasting memories of happiness and joy, building a strong emotional connection that withstands the test of time. It's the principle of building a skyscraper of habits and a tower of memories that can withstand the seismic events of life.

Let's be cognizant that it might not always be smooth sailing, but I believe that a good old smile can enhance your communication and conflict-resolution skills in your intimate relationship. During challenging times, a smile can diffuse tension and soften the impact of difficult conversations. It shows that you are willing to approach issues with empathy and a positive mindset, inviting your partner to open up, share their thoughts, and work towards resolution together, find common ground and strengthening your emotional bond.

Bring playfulness and spontaneity into your romantic relationship, send the signal for shared experiences and adventures by using your smile to initiate fun and joyful activities, create opportunities for bonding and creating new memories together. After all it's one of those ingredients that does not cost you a penny. So, go ahead and apply this game-changing technique to build a strong foundation of love and happiness, fostering a fulfilling romantic journey with your partner.

It is truly a game changer and a remarkable asset in your life endeavors. It holds the power to make a lasting impression, foster connections, and create a positive and productive environment. You can amplify your professional image, communicate effectively, build networks, and ultimately open doors to new opportunities. Wear your smile proudly as a guiding light in your career journey, embracing grace and positivity.

If you are looking to enhance your professional image, break the ice, and build rapport, lean on the power of a genuine smile, it can instantly create a warm and welcoming atmosphere, making others feel comfortable and at ease in your presence, projects, enhance your self-assurance and professionalism. It shows that you take pride in your work and radiate a positive attitude, which can enhance your credibility and reputation. A well-timed smile can make you appear more approachable, confident, and competent, leaving a lasting impression on others.

Our most pleasant face will radiate a smile that can act as a gateway to gratitude and happiness, it can demonstrate a shift in focus towards the positive aspects of life. Our smile reinforces our feelings of happiness, deepening our experience of gratitude and enhancing our overall sense of well-being.

CHAPTER 10

THE SMILE FROM A HEART OF LOVE

Powerful expressions that a person can make is yet to be summarized and put under one umbrella, but most of the time, what is put forward can express an emotion of joy, happiness, and contentment. But it can also be a sign of something much deeper. When a person smiles, it can be an indication that they are radiating a heart of love and compassion. A heartwarming smile can profoundly impact a person's face and offer comfort during emotional distress.

The beauty of a smile that radiates from a heart of love is that it can often have a transformative effect on a person's face. Not only does it make them appear more attractive, but it can also change the way a person feels. A smile can make a person look more vibrant and alive and can even be a source of strength in difficult times. Smiling can be a way to show that you care and that you are there for someone. It can also be an effective way to express your feelings to someone without having to say a word.

A smile that radiates from a heart of love is truly one of the greatest beauties to behold. It is said that a smile can be seen in the eyes, and it is easy to see why. A smile of genuine love and joy gives a special kind of life to your face and brings joy to those around you. It is something that can be seen in many ways. It brings out the best in your face, highlighting the natural beauty that lies within. It brings brightness to your eyes and a glow to your cheeks. This is the beauty that's visible from a distance.

But the beauty of a smile radiating from a heart of love is so much more than just physical beauty. It is a kind of beauty that brings peace and joy to those around you. It is the kind of beauty that encourages those around you to smile. It is the kind of beauty that can be shared and passed on to others, allowing them to enjoy the same joy and peace that you are feeling.

"Just magical if you ask me."

I believe there are some benefits that are far-reaching. This magical transfer can help to relieve stress and anxiety and boost your self-confidence. One may ask, how about relationships? Oh yeah! Just one look at that face can change a lot. That smile is one of the most beautiful gifts to behold. It radiates from a heart of love and brings joy to everyone who sees it. The beauty of a smile can be seen in the way it lights up the face, making it brighter and more cheerful. So, of course! It can improve your relationships, making you more likely to take risks and take on new challenges. It can even help you to be more productive and successful.

A smile from a heart of love is often contagious, making even the grumpiest of people smile in return. It is a sign of happiness, joy, and of contentment. When someone smiles, it shows that their heart is full of love and that they are truly glad. Overall, it can have a positive effect on our physical appearance, help us look younger, healthier, reduce stress, and help keep wrinkles at bay. It is truly a blessing in disguise and can brighten someone's day, spreading joy throughout the world. Take it as a true sign of happiness, contentment, acceptance and understanding. This smile is a powerful thing whose beauty is timeless. The next time you encounter someone with a sincere, heartfelt smile, pause for a moment to appreciate the beauty it carries. Let it fill your heart with joy and serve as a reminder of the profound and impactful power of love and human connection.

A smile that radiates from a heart of love also has the power to make someone else's day brighter. Even a simple gesture like smiling can make someone's day a little bit better. It can be a sign of support and understanding and can even be a source of hope in tough times. Smiling is contagious, so even if you are feeling hurt or emotional distress, you can still spread a little bit of joy. You never know - it may just be the thing that changes someone's day. The power of a smile can be a magnificent tool for conveying emotion, and when it radiates from a heart of love, its beauty can be truly transformative. In a society that often values external appearances, a smile can be a powerful reminder to stay focused on what truly matters - our innermost feelings and thoughts. But what about those moments when our feelings are deeply wounded? How do we benefit from a smile during times of distress when we find ourselves in an uncontrolled state of consciousness? How can a smile help us in such situations?

The answer lies in the thought process. When we're feeling hurt or distressed, our thoughts tend to be dominated by negative emotions, such as fear or sadness. But when we smile, we're actively changing the thought process by bringing in positive emotions. We're actively encouraging ourselves to focus on the good things in life and to be grateful for our blessings.

This can help us to break free from negative thought patterns and to find peace and happiness in the present moment. Creating that beautiful outward expression is not just a mere physical gesture; it is an expression that originates from the depths of our inner self. When a smile is fueled by love, it becomes a powerful and transformative force, radiating positivity and beauty to the environment.

"It involves a profound thought process and an inner state of being that can create a truly remarkable outward expression, especially on our faces."

It begins with cultivating a deep sense of inner love and compassion, appreciating the beauty of our own existence, recognizing our inherent worth, and extending that love to others. It's a good punchline, when we genuinely love ourselves and have an abundance of love to share, by default, our smiles become genuine and authentic, a mirror reflection of that inner love.

How is that for a default face?

"I'll take it."

"The thought process behind a smile that originates from a loving heart is rooted in mindfulness and awareness."

It's the principle of becoming cognizant and having the volition to push through and take action, it's being present in the moment, observing our thoughts, and consciously "choosing love" as the foundation of our actions. This often requires us to let go of negative emotions, judgments, and allowing love to guide our interactions with others. With a strong determination to cultivate positive thoughts, focus on inner goodness, and appreciating others, we may create the fertile environment for a smile to blossom. When a smile emerges from a heart filled with love, it manifests as a beautiful outward expression. It has the power to light up our faces, transforming our features into windows that reflect the radiance we have within us.

"A smile that emanates from love is contagious,
spreading joy and warmth to everyone who encounters it."

It has the ability to dissolve barriers and unite people in a shared experience of positivity and connection. It invites others to open their hearts, creating a ripple effect of love and kindness. This magical facial expression has a profound impact on both the giver and the receiver.

Firstly, it uplifts our own spirits creating a unique vibe of inner peace and solace. Take note: if our heart is in the right place, the smile that we exhibit makes us agents of transformation, bringing light into the lives of others we encounter.

A smile that stems from a heart filled with love becomes a powerful tool for healing and transformation. It reminds us of the inherent goodness that exists within us and invites us to see the same goodness in others, serves as a beacon of hope, and a gentle reminder that a smile conveying love can overcome any darkness, one heartfelt expression at a time.

Let's fuel the smile testosterone, build a skyscraper of healthy habits, and a tower of fond memories. It can have an appealing physical impact on our appearance, sculpting smiling muscles to relax our faces, and producing a look that is cheerful, and relaxed, and giving your face a rest.

The beauty of a smile that radiates from a heart of love, a heart that is glad, can be truly transformative and bring much cheer. It can have a powerful effect on both our internal and external states. The smile that radiates from a heart filled with love is a beautiful and genuine expression of our innermost thoughts and emotions. This type of smile transcends superficiality; it's a reflection of the deep-seated feelings of affection, compassion, and warmth that reside within us. It is a symbol of the positive thoughts and attitudes that we cultivate, which are greatly influenced by our habits and lifestyle.

"Our daily habits and the way we choose to live our lives play
a pivotal role in nurturing the kind of love and positivity
that can manifest as this radiant smile."

When we practice habits of gratitude, mindfulness, and kindness, we create an inner environment that is conducive to love and joy. These habits encourage us to focus on the positive aspects of life, foster empathy for others, and appreciate beauty in even the simplest situations. Over time, these practices shape our thoughts, guiding them toward more loving and positive perspectives. Our lifestyle choices further influence our capacity to generate this heartwarming smile. Surrounding ourselves with nurturing relationships, engaging in activities that bring us joy, and prioritizing self-care all contribute to a life filled with love and positivity. When we are content, fulfilled, and at peace with ourselves, it becomes easier to project that inner happiness outward. Our faces naturally light up with a genuine smile that radiates warmth and love, creating a beautiful and contagious expression that can brighten the lives of those around us.

In essence, the smile that radiates from a heart of love is a testament to the power of our thoughts, habits, and lifestyle choices. It reflects the inner beauty that blossoms when we cultivate a positive, loving mindset and a life that aligns with these values. This kind of smile not only transforms our own well-being but also serves as a beacon of positivity and inspiration to those fortunate enough to witness it.

Let's actively encourage ourselves to smile and to focus on the positive, we can break free from negative thought patterns and find peace and happiness. You may never get a chance to see it, but your default face will thank you for it.

INSPIRATIONAL IMAGERY

With just one jot of inspiration, you could change the world.

*"Journal your thoughts? Oh! Just thought I would ask. Build a
skyscraper of healthy habits."*
~~ Inspired ~~.
L. A. Chambers

*"Habit is a noun that exhibits from one's attitude, but attitude is
the noun that exhibits one's inner thoughts and feelings."*
~~ Inspired ~~.
L. A. Chambers

*"Build a tower of memories that will withstand emotional
turbulence and dissipate seismically induced events of life."*
~~ Inspired ~~.
L. A. Chambers

*"Knowledge and understanding are ingredients to prosperity,
but cognizance is the volition. Sow choices that make you reap
joy."*
~~ Inspired ~~.
L. A. Chambers

ABOUT THE AUTHOR

L. A. CHAMBERS is a seasoned professional leader with a
wealth of corporate experience. Having obtained multiple
professional designations, he has now embarked on a journey
as an inspirational writer. Chambers also has a love
for music and art, which has allowed him to
touch lives with harmonies of love.

During a transformative period, Chambers discovered the
profound impact of cognizance and volition, which propelled
him towards his current path as an inspirational writer.
His unwavering commitment to inspiring and
motivating others are rooted in the belief that a life filled with
love, happiness, and success leads to genuine fulfillment.
With his diverse background and deep understanding of human
potential, Chambers is a powerful catalyst for positive change.

Journal Your Thoughts?

The White Paper: Build a skyscraper of healthy habits.

Any Takeaways from This Book?

Don't leave knowledge on the table.
Jot them here.

Any Takeaways from This Book?

Don't leave knowledge on the table.
Jot them here.